# MySQL Replication Simplified

## Sribatsa Das, MBA

ii

# About the Author

Sribatsa Das holds a Bachelors and Masters in Computer Science. He holds an MBA from New York University's Leonard N. Stern School of Business in Finance and Strategy.

Sribatsa's passion is technology. He strives at bringing technological innovative products to life every day leveraging his long technology career and finance education. Sribatsa started as a DBA and application developer in his early career. After 20+ years long stint in IT and consulting, he embarked upon entrepreneurship

He launched Business Compass® LLC mobile app start-up venture in 2008. This start-up has launched 200+ mobile apps. MBA Sidekick, Mobile Statistics Professor® and Altman Z-Score+ are his key innovations. MBA Sidekick offers a full array of analytical tools to MBA students and professionals. MBA Statistics Professor provides tools to carry out college and MBA level statistical analysis. Altman Z-Score+ analyzes credit risk of companies worldwide including bond rating equivalent and up to 10 years of default probability. This product is available on leading financial data terminal via APPS ALTMAN <GO> command.

Business Compass LLC's web sites are http://businesscompassllc.com and http://altmanzscoreplus.com. Sribatsa can be contacted via e-mail at sribatsa.das@businesscompassllc.com.

Additional information about this book can be found at http://mysqlreplicationsimplified.com. Training is available to purchase at http://businesscompassllc.com/training.

# Preface

I worked with many databases during my long technology career. I implemented ERP, CRM and Data Warehousing Systems. MySQL is a wonderful database. MySQL offers great replication capabilities. While the process to establish replication is straight forward, in reality many problems arise. When errors are encountered, the answers many; however, are not very simple or clear. I got lost in the forest while establishing MySQL replication for large transactional databases running round the clock. I spent countless hours reviewing the existing literature to find solutions to the errors that does not connect the dots.  That compelled me to write this book to share my experience so that establishing replication does not become an odyssey. This book provides numerous visuals and examples to simplify the concepts to establish effective replication as well as to make repairing a broken replication system easy. My goal of writing this book is to provide simple solution to various replication configurations and remedy to common problems so that the reader can establish and troubleshoot MySQL replication issues effortlessly.

## Table of Contents

x

# 1   What is MySQL Replication

Replication is a process to copy data from one database to another synchronously to keep the same copy of the replicating system on the replicated system. The replicating database is commonly known as "master" and the replicated database is commonly known as "slave". MySQL introduced replication before the millennium. Around the same time frame MySQL gained popularity as part of the LAMP (Linux-Apache-MySQL-PHP) stack. Today, MySQL commands the position of the second most popular open source databases. It has closed the ranks with the modern RDBMS systems commercially available.

MySQL offers robust replication mechanism. Bi-directional two master, master-slave, master slave with changed slaves, circular multi-master replication configurations are available. By utilizing the replication functionality high available, failover can be designed. Replication can be utilized for real-time backup of a transactional system where downtime required to perform an off-line backup is not possible. Reporting is a constant requirement from demanding business users to run business. Due to conflicting performance requirement, a reporting system is highly desirable. Replication offers capability to build a copy of production database and to keep it synch with production real-time to allow users to generate most up-to-date reports from the replicated reporting system.

This book progresses as follows progressively elaborating the concepts.

Chapter 2 – Benefits of replication
Chapter 3 – How replication process works
Chapter 4 – Replication configurations
Chapter 5- Components of Replication system
Chapter 6 – Approach to replication
Chapter 7 – Copying master to replica
Chapter 8 – MySQL configuration parameters
Chapter 9 – Commands useful to establish replication
Chapter 10 – Setting up of replication user account
Chapter 11-17 – Establishing various replication configurations
Chapter 18 – Skipping SQL Errors
Chapter 19 – Using SQL_Slave_Skip_Counter to fix replication
Chapter 20 – Experimenting with auto increment variables
Chapter 21 – Interpreting show slave status output
Chapter 22 – Understanding show processlist
Chapter 23 – Including & excluding databases & tables in replication
Chapter 24 – Interpreting binary and relay log files using mysqlbinlog
Chapter 25 – Troubleshooting and repairing broken replication
Chapter 26 – Monitoring MySQL replication

Linux system is primarily used in the examples.  Commands are italicized. Plenty of examples are presented to assimilate the concepts.

# 2  What are the Benefits of replication

This chapter explains the benefits of replication. Replication can offer high-availability including load balancing and failover.  Replication can be used to create effective real-time backup. Replication can also be used to create reporting database for querying.

## 2.1  High Availability

High available system offers performance via load balancing and failover benefits.

### 2.1.1  Load Balancing

Modern application can support a large number of users. Users often demand split second response time from the transactional systems. In order to support these non-functional or performance requirements, load balancing may need to be implemented. In a load balancing configuration more than one database server is deployed. Depending upon the user load on one server, the users are diverted to the other server. To keep a single point of truth of data, replication is away to keep the databases in synchronization so that all the database servers contain the same copy of the data at a given time to reduce data inconsistency for transactions. A load balancing architecture is presented in Figure 2-1. In this scenario, *master-high level master active-active* replication can be established. More about this will be discussed in chapter 4.

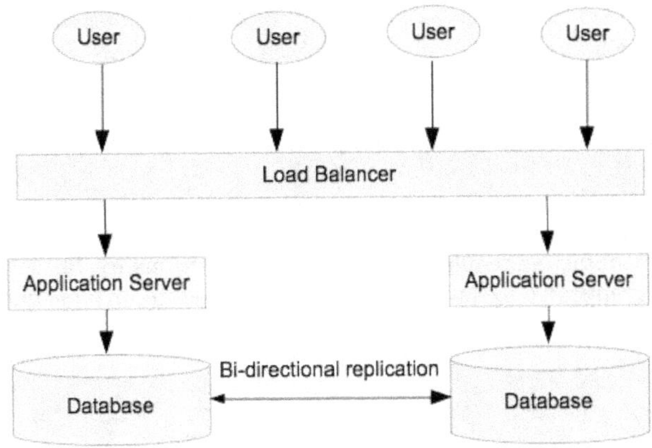


Figure 2—1: Load Balancing Architecture

### 2.1.2  Failover

Similar to load balancing, high availability is a requirement for applications running 24x7 365 days a year. A master can be replicated to another master so that if the replicating master fails, the replicated master can take place of the replicating master and the application can continue to running. Failover may or may not be automatic.  A high-level failover mechanism is presented in Figure 2-2.

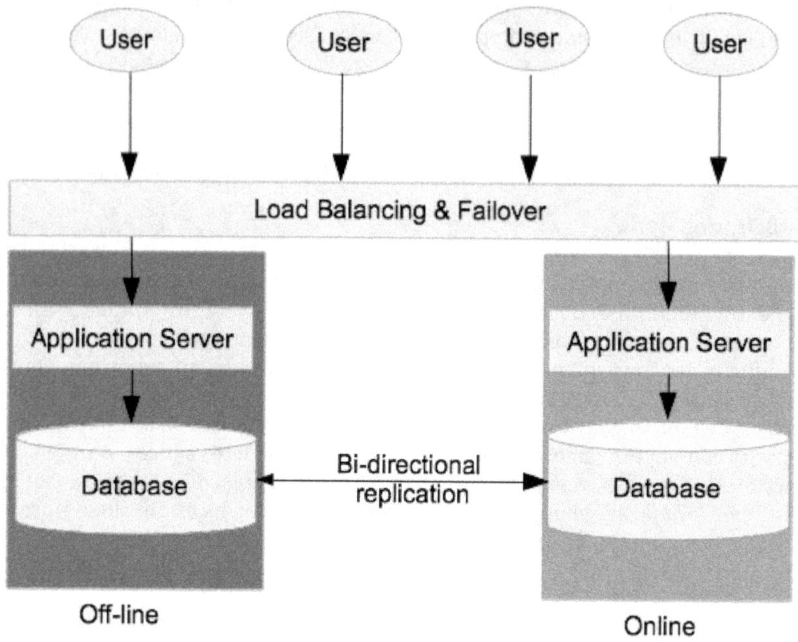


Figure 2—2: Failover Architecture

## 2.2   Reporting

Users often require reporting and analysis of production data. Transaction processing and reporting are mutually conflicting requirements for system performance. In such scenarios, production database is replicated to slave. The users are allowed to run large queries and reports on the slave.  A high level reporting architecture is presented in Figure 2-3.

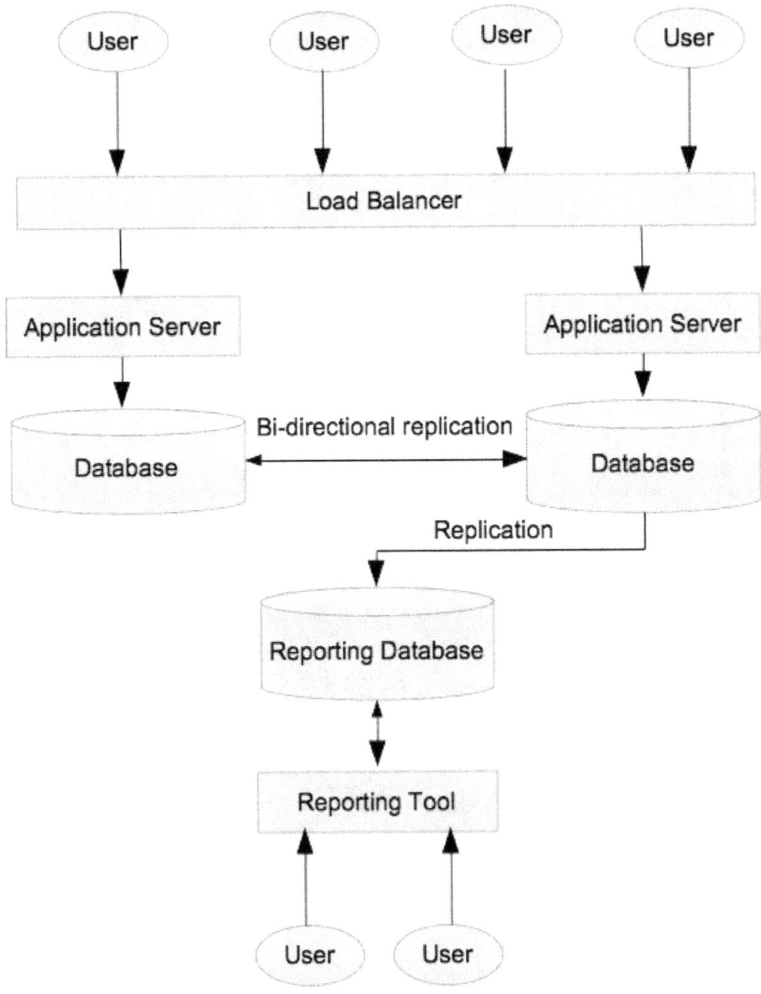


Figure 2—3: Reporting Architecture

## 2.3  Backup

Backup provides a mechanism to protect against catastrophic failure. Database backup and recovery is broadly governed by

- Recovery Time Objective – How long will the recovery process take?
- Recovery Point Objective – Up to what point in time the recovery can be performed.

5

Modern systems often run 24x7 365 days a year running transactional database No time is available for off-line backup or file system copy or mysqldump In such scenarios, replication offers an effective real-time backup which allows point-in-time recovery.

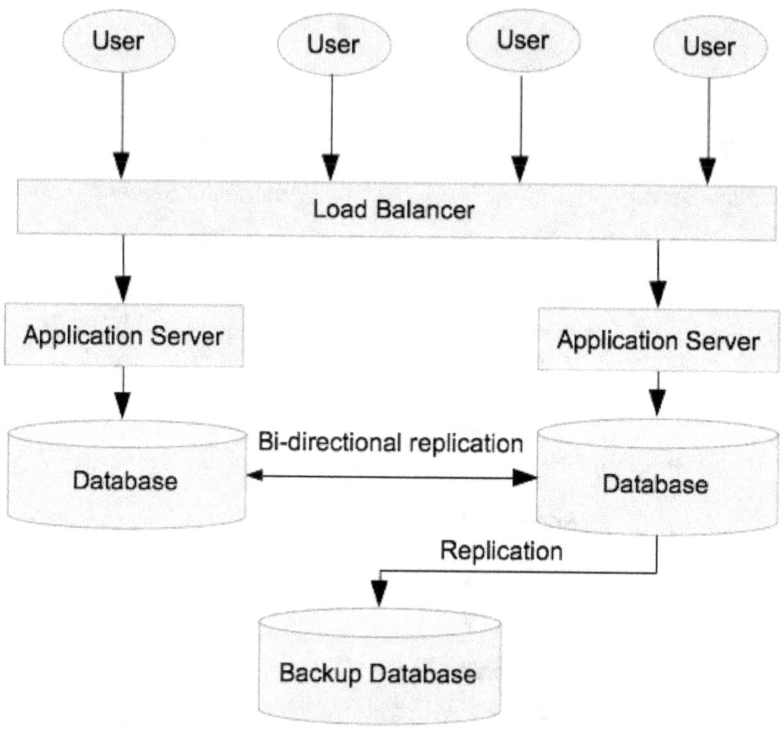


Figure 2—4: Backup Architecture

## 2.4   Summary

This chapter presented the benefits of replication.

# 3   How Replication Works

A replication system consists of a master and a slave. Master writes log events to its binary log. The slave reads master's binary log transactions and applies the log events on its databases.

Each master-slave configuration starts 3 threads – 2 running on the slave and one running on the master. The two slaves started on slave are I/O thread and SQL thread. The one started on master is Binlog dump thread.

When *start slave* command is executed on the slave, slave starts I/O thread and SQL When the I/O thread connects to the master, the master creates Binlog dump thread. The Binlog dump thread locks the binary log on master, reads the log events, releases the lock and sends the events to the slave I/O thread. The slave I/O thread writes the master's log events to the slave's relay log file. The slave SQL thread reads the relay log file and replays the master's log events on the slave databases. Then, the cycle of master's Binlog dump reading master binary log for log events, sending the log events to slave I/O, slave writing to slave's relay log, slave SQL thread reading the relay log and replaying the event on slave continues.  This is illustrated in the following diagram.

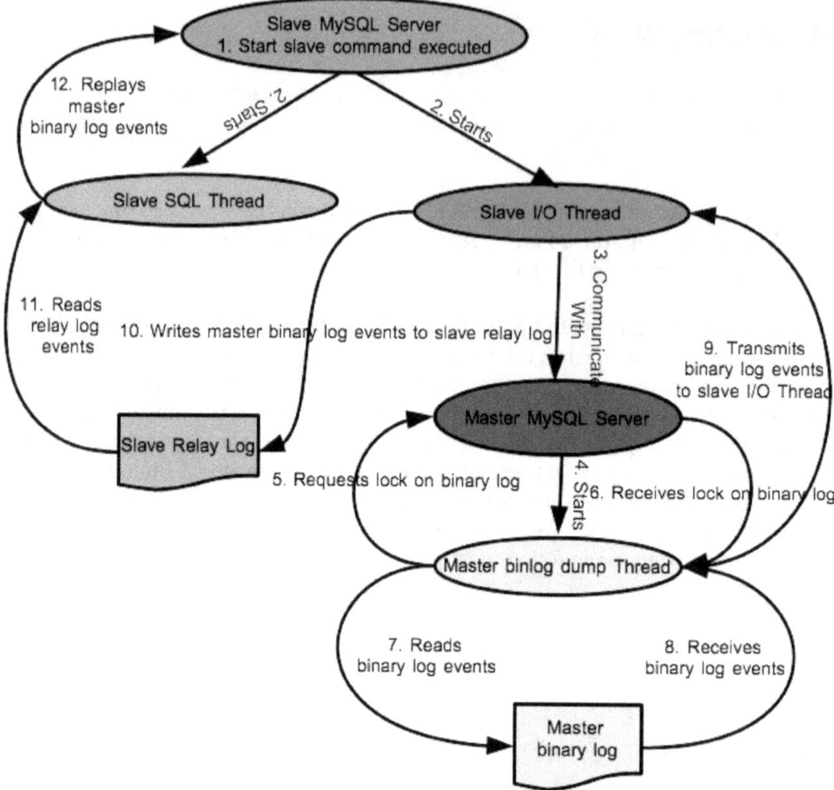


Figure 3—1: Replication Threads

### 3.1.1   Master Binary log dump Thread

When a slave's I/O thread connects to master, master starts this thread to read master's binary log events to send to slave I/O process.

### 3.1.2   Slave I/O Thread

Slave I/O thread starts when the *start slave* command is executed on the slave.

### 3.1.3   SQL Thread

When *start slave* command is executed, this thread is started.

The sequence of events to make replication operation is as follows.

- *Show master status* executed on master to read master's log coordinates

- *Change master* command is executed on slave to provide master coordinates to slave
- *Start slave* is executed on slave to start slave processes

*Show master status* executed on master to read master's log coordinates. A screenshot of the executed command is presented below.

```
mysql> show master status;
+------------------+----------+--------------+------------------+
| File             | Position | Binlog_Do_DB | Binlog_Ignore_DB |
+------------------+----------+--------------+------------------+
| mysql-bin.000009 |      106 |              |                  |
+------------------+----------+--------------+------------------+
1 row in set (0.00 sec)
```

**Screen-shot 3—1: show master status on master server mobilestatisticsprofessor.us**

*Show processlist* is executed on slave to verify what processes are running on slave.

```
mysql> show processlist\g
+----+------+-----------+------+---------+------+-------+------------------+
| Id | User | Host      | db   | Command | Time | State | Info             |
+----+------+-----------+------+---------+------+-------+------------------+
|  8 | root | localhost | NULL | Query   |    0 | NULL  | show processlist |
+----+------+-----------+------+---------+------+-------+------------------+
1 row in set (0.00 sec)
```

**Screen-shot 3—2: show processlist output on master server mobilestatisticsprofessor.us**

*Change master* command issued on slave and tart slave command executed on slave

```
mysql> change master to master_host='mobilestatisticsprofessor.us', master_user='repl', master
 password='velcro20', master_log_file='mysql-bin.000009', master_log_pos=106;
Query OK, 0 rows affected (0.16 sec)

mysql> start slave;
Query OK, 0 rows affected (0.01 sec)
```

**Screen-shot 3—3: change master and start slave commands executed on slave server mobilestatisticsprofessor.com**

*Show processlist* is executed on slave. Two new processes appear – one waiting for master to send event that is the slave I/O process and another waiting for slave I/O to update relay log that is the slave SQL thread.

```
mysql> show processlist\G
*************************** 1. row ***************************
     Id: 8
   User: root
   Host: localhost
     db: NULL
Command: Query
   Time: 0
  State: NULL
   Info: show processlist
*************************** 2. row ***************************
     Id: 9
   User: system user
   Host:
     db: NULL
Command: Connect
   Time: 11
  State: Waiting for master to send event
   Info: NULL
*************************** 3. row ***************************
     Id: 10
   User: system user
   Host:
     db: NULL
Command: Connect
   Time: 10
  State: Has read all relay log; waiting for the slave I/O thread to update it
   Info: NULL
3 rows in set (0.00 sec)
```

**Screen-shot 3—4: show processlist output on slave server mobilestatisticsprofessor.com**

Show slave status will provide further details of slave threads. In screenshot 3.5, Slave I/O State is waiting for master to send event. I/O thread read up to position 106 of log file mysql-bin.000009 that is depicted by two variables in the show master status output.

Master_Log_File: mysql-bin.000009
Read_Master_log_Pos: 106

SQL Thread executed up to position 106 in master log file mysql-bin.000009 that is depicted by two variables

Relay_Master_Log_File: mysql-bin.000009
Exec_Master_log_Pos: 106

Therefore, the slave I/O and SQL threads have applied master binary log to slave.

Slave SQL thread does not read directly from master's binary log. It reads from slave's relay log file. Slave SQL thread read relay log file mysqld-relay-bin.00002 and up to position 243.

Relay_ Log_File: mysqld-relay-bin.00002
Relay_log_Pos: 243

```
mysql> show slave status\G
*************************** 1. row ***************************
               Slave_IO_State: Waiting for master to send event
                  Master_Host: mobilestatisticsprofessor.us
                  Master_User: repl
                  Master_Port: 3306
                Connect_Retry: 60
              Master_Log_File: mysql-bin.000009
          Read_Master_Log_Pos: 106
               Relay_Log_File: mysqld-relay-bin.000002
                Relay_Log_Pos: 243
        Relay_Master_Log_File: mysql-bin.000009
             Slave_IO_Running: Yes
            Slave_SQL_Running: Yes
              Replicate_Do_DB:
          Replicate_Ignore_DB:
           Replicate_Do_Table:
       Replicate_Ignore_Table:
      Replicate_Wild_Do_Table:
  Replicate_Wild_Ignore_Table:
                   Last_Errno: 0
                   Last_Error:
                 Skip_Counter: 0
          Exec_Master_Log_Pos: 106
              Relay_Log_Space: 243
              Until_Condition: None
               Until_Log_File:
                Until_Log_Pos: 0
           Master_SSL_Allowed: No
           Master_SSL_CA_File:
           Master_SSL_CA_Path:
              Master_SSL_Cert:
            Master_SSL_Cipher:
               Master_SSL_Key:
        Seconds_Behind_Master: 0
1 row in set (0.00 sec)
```

**Screen-shot 3—5: show slave status output on slave server mobilestatisticsprofessor.com**

On master, *show processlist* is executed. The Binlog Dump process appears.

```
mysql> show processlist\G
*************************** 1. row ***************************
     Id: 3
   User: root
   Host: localhost
     db: NULL
Command: Query
   Time: 0
  State: NULL
   Info: show processlist
*************************** 2. row ***************************
     Id: 4
   User: repl
   Host: ip-72-167-246-49.ip.secureserver.net:60405
     db: NULL
Command: Binlog Dump
   Time: 58
  State: Has sent all binlog to slave; waiting for binlog to be updated
   Info: NULL
2 rows in set (0.00 sec)
```

**Screen-shot 3—6: output of show processlist executed on the master mobilestatisticsprofessor.us after starting slave on mobilestatisticsprofessor.com**

## 3.2  Summary

This chapter explained how replication works and what role the threads play on master and slave.

# 4   MySQL Replication Configurations

MySQL Support multiple configurations. Bi-directional replication can be established between two master servers. Circular replication can be established among multiple masters. Master can replicate to multiple slaves. A slave can replicate to other slaves as a master. However, a slave cannot be replicated from multiple masters. A permutation of allowable replication topology is presented below.

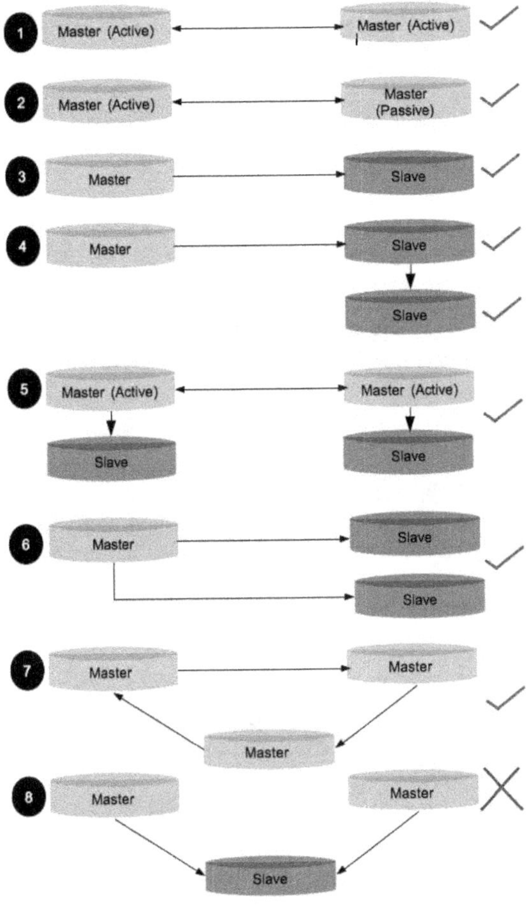


Figure 4—1: Replication Configurations

## 4.1   Allowed Configurations

### 4.1.1   Master-Master
Bi-directional replication can be established between two masters. Each master can allow transactions to take place; thus be active for the purpose of transactions. A master can be placed in read only mode; thus becoming passive for transaction purpose.

#### *4.1.1.1   Active-Active*

If both the masters allow transactions, then each master becomes active for transaction. This configuration is known as Master-Master-Active-Active. Chapter 11 presents this configuration.

#### *4.1.1.2   Active-Passive*
If a master does not allow user transactions, then the master becomes passive for transactional purposes.  This configuration is known as Master-Master-Active-Passive. Chapter 12 presents this configuration.


### 4.1.2   Master-Slave

When a master is replicating to a slave, the configuration is known as master-slave. This configuration is widely used. Chapter 13 presents this configuration.


### 4.1.3   Master-Slave-Slave Chain

A master can replicate to a slave. A slave can replicate to another slave in a chain when log_slave_updates and log_bin are turned on the slave replicating directly from the master. The chain of slaves replicating to other slaves can be extended.   Chapter 14 presents this configuration.


### 4.1.4   Master-Slaves

A master can replicate to multiple slaves. In such configuration, each slave can further replicate to its slaves. Chapter 15 presents this configuration.


### 4.1.5   Master-Master-Master Circular

Multiple masters can participate in replication in a circular fashion. Three masters A, B and C can participate as A to B to C to A replication configuration. Four masters A, B, C, D can replicate in A to B to C to D to A configuration.  Chapter 16 presents this configuration.

### 4.1.6   Master-Master-Slave-Slave

Each master in a master-master replication configuration can replicate to slaves of its own. In such configuration, each slave can further replicate to its slaves. Chapter 17 presents this configuration.

## 4.2   Prohibited Configuration

Two or more masters cannot replicate to a slave since a slave can read the binary log of only one master at a time. However, the reverse is possible where one master can replicate to multiple slaves.

# 5   Components of Replication System

This chapter describes what constitutes the replication system. Replicating master logs events in its binary log. Binlog dump thread in master sends the log events to the slave's I/O thread, which are in turn read by slave's SQL thread and applied to slave's databases. This chapter describes the configuration parameters, file system and threads both on master and slave. A bird's eye view of the processes and file system is presented below.

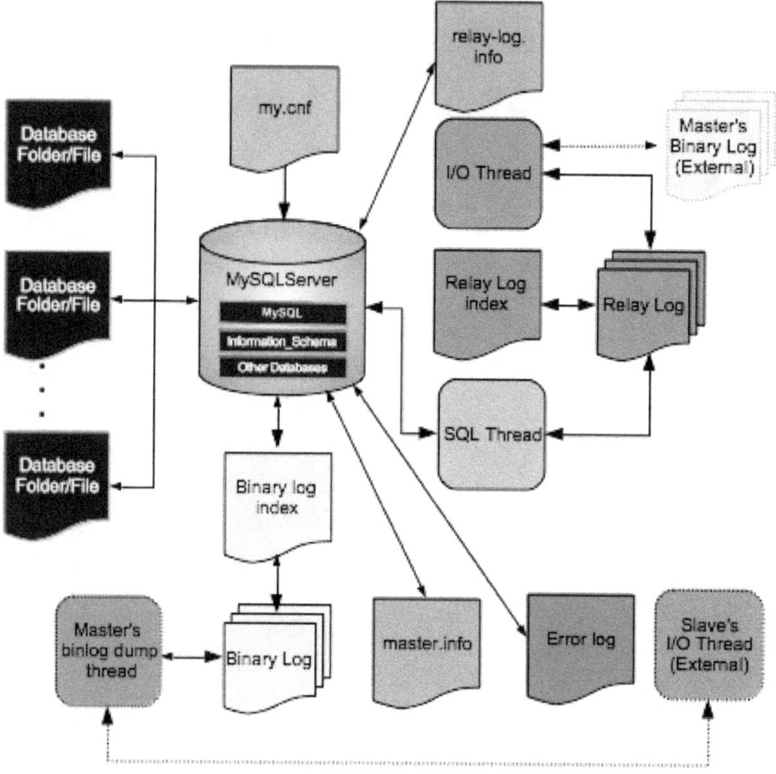


Figure 5—1: Components of Replication System

## 5.1   Directory structure

The data directory, base directory and error log directories for a running MySQL server can be obtained from the *ps –eaf | grep mysqld* command in Unix.  A screenshot of the output is provided below.

```
[root@ip-72-167-246-49 ~]# ps -eaf | grep mysqld
root     13456 13420  0 06:07 pts/0    00:00:00 grep mysqld
root     26125     1  0 May12 ?        00:00:00 /bin/sh /usr/bin/mysqld_safe --datadir=/var/li
b/mysql --socket=/var/lib/mysql/mysql.sock --log-error=/var/log/mysqld.log --pid-file=/var/run
/mysqld/mysqld.pid --user=mysql
mysql    26175 26125  0 May12 ?        00:02:34 /usr/libexec/mysqld --basedir=/usr --datadir=/
var/lib/mysql --user=mysql --pid-file=/var/run/mysqld/mysqld.pid --skip-external-locking --soc
ket=/var/lib/mysql/mysql.sock
```

**Screen-shot 5—1: Output of ps –eaf | grep mysqld command executed on Linux command prompt**

In the above screenshot the data directory is /var/lib/mysql. Directory listing on /var/lib/mysql generates the following.

```
[root@mob mysql]# ls
                  master.info                              mysqld-relay-bin.000005
changemaster.sql  mob.mobilestatisticsprofessor.us.err    mysqld-relay-bin.index
grant.sql
                  mysql-bin.000001
ibdata1           mysql-bin.000002
ib_logfile0       mysql-bin.index
ib_logfile1       mysqld-relay-bin.000004                  relay-log.info
[root@mob mysql]#
```

**Screen-shot 5—2: Output of ls command executed on mysql home directory**

The replication related files are as follows from the above screenshot.
- mysql-bin.index is the binary log index.
- mysql-bin.000001 and mysql-bin.000002 are the binary log files.
- mysqld-relay-bin.index is the relay log index.
- mysqld-relay-bin.000004 and mysqld-relay-bin.000005 are the relay log files.
- master.info is the file that contains information about the master server. This file does not exist until change master command is issued and slave is started. This file is deleted when reset slave command is issued.
- relay-log.info contains the position of the last executed binary log in slave against the master binary log position.

## 5.2   my.cnf

MySQL uses a configuration file to start the server. Below is a screenshot of a my.cnf file.

```
[mysqld]
local-infile=0
max_allowed_packet=16M
set-variable=local-infile=0
datadir=/var/lib/mysql
socket=/var/lib/mysql/mysql.sock
user=mysql
# Default to using old password format for compatibility with mysql 3.x
# clients (those using the mysqlclient10 compatibility package).
old_passwords=1

log_bin=/var/lib/mysql/mysql-bin.log
server_id=1
expire_logs_days=1
# Disabling symbolic-links is recommended to prevent assorted security risks;
# to do so, uncomment this line:
# symbolic-links=0

#skip-bdb

innodb_buffer_pool_size=2M
innodb_additional_mem_pool_size=500K
innodb_log_buffer_size=500K
innodb_thread_concurrency=2
[mysqld_safe]
log-error=/var/log/mysqld.log
pid-file=/var/run/mysqld/mysqld.pid
#skip-bdb

innodb_buffer_pool_size=2M
innodb_additional_mem_pool_size=500K
innodb_log_buffer_size=500K
innodb_thread_concurrency=2
```

**Screen-shot 5—3: Sample my.cnf file**

Replication related parameters present in the my.cnf file are as follows:

**server_id:** Server id is a mandatory parameter for a server to participate in a replication configuration either as a master or a slave. This parameter contains a numeric value specified after the equal sign. This number needs to be unique for each server participating in a replication topology. If the server_id value is not unique, then the replication slave cannot be started successfully.

**Log_bin:** if this line is specified, then the server starts in a binary log mode or starts logging transactions in binary log. If this line is commented out (by placing a # in the front of the line) or the line is absent altogether, then the server starts in a non-binary logging mode. For the server to replicate to another or become master of other servers, the server needs to start in the binary logging mode. Optionally, the location and format of binary log file name can be specified. This can be specified to the right of the equal sign after log_bin. Log_bin with or without the file path and format must be specified in the master for replication to occur.

**Expire_log_days:** This parameters specifies after how many days logs will be recycled.

**Log_slave_updates:** This parameters makes a slave to log updates performed by its SQL thread. Log_bin option must be specified for log_slave_updates to become effective.

**Read_only:** This option makes the server to update only from slave thread or from users with SUPER privileges. No user updates are permitted. This ensures that the slave is in synch with the master and no other process breaks the data consistency in the slave.

**Slave_skip_errors:** This option allows SQL thread to by-pass certain SQL errors and keep the SQL Thread running. Without this option, the SQL thread will stop if the slave encounters a SQL error. By using this option, certain SQL errors can be by-passed.

**Relay_log:** This option can be specified to provide a directory location of the relay log and the format of the relay log files.

**Auto_increment_increment and auto_increment_offset**: in a multi-master replication scenario to preserve the value of unique or primary keys which are set up to derive value through auto_increment when data is inserted to the key value in a table, setting auto_increment_increment and auto_increment_offset allows unique key values to be generated across the master servers and thus, avoid collision of auto_increment value.

Auto_increment_increment should be the same as the number of master servers. Auto_increment_offset should be any integer between 1 and the number of servers.

## 5.3   error log

MySQL writes messages and errors beginning with starting MySQL Server until the server is shutdown. From a replication perspective, whether slave started correctly or any SQL or I/O thread error occurred should monitored to ensure smooth replication operation. A screenshot of an error log is provided below.

```
140511  3:38:38 [Note] Error reading relay log event: slave SQL thread was kille
d
140511  3:57:35 [Note] Slave SQL thread initialized, starting replication in log
 'mysql-bin.000002' at position 2262, relay log './mysqld-relay-bin.000001' posi
tion: 4
140511  3:57:35 [Note] Slave I/O thread: connected to master 'repl@mobilestatist
icsprofessor.us:3306',  replication started in log 'mysql-bin.000002' at positio
n 2262
140511  4:43:39 [Note] Slave I/O thread killed while reading event
140511  4:43:39 [Note] Slave I/O thread exiting, read up to log 'mysql-bin.00000
2', position 2262
140511  4:43:39 [Note] Error reading relay log event: slave SQL thread was kille
d
140512  5:35:57 [Note] /usr/libexec/mysqld: Normal shutdown

140512  5:35:57  InnoDB: Starting shutdown...
140512  5:36:05  InnoDB: Shutdown completed; log sequence number 0 407122417
140512  5:36:05 [Note] /usr/libexec/mysqld: Shutdown complete

140512 05:36:05  mysqld ended

140512 05:36:06  mysqld started
140512  5:36:06 [Warning] option 'max_join_size': unsigned value 184467440737095
51615 adjusted to 4294967295
140512  5:36:06 [Warning] option 'max_join_size': unsigned value 184467440737095
51615 adjusted to 4294967295
140512  5:36:16  InnoDB: Started; log sequence number 0 407122417
140512  5:36:18 [Note] /usr/libexec/mysqld: ready for connections.
Version: '5.0.77-log'  socket: '/var/lib/mysql/mysql.sock'  port: 3306  Source d
istribution
140512  5:36:18 [Note] Slave SQL thread initialized, starting replication in log
 'mysql-bin.000002' at position 2262, relay log './mysqld-relay-bin.000002' posi
tion: 243
140512  5:36:18 [Note] Slave I/O thread: connected to master 'repl@mobilestatist
icsprofessor.us:3306',  replication started in log 'mysql-bin.000002' at positio
n 2262
140512  5:36:19 [ERROR] Slave: Error 'Table 't' already exists' on query. Defaul
t database: 'test'. Query: 'create table t (id int, pid int)', Error_code: 1050
140512  5:36:19 [ERROR] Error running query, slave SQL thread aborted. Fix the p
roblem, and restart the slave SQL thread with "SLAVE START". We stopped at log '
mysql-bin.000002' position 2262
```

Screen-shot 5—4: Excerpt from MySQL Error Log

## 5.4   binary log index

This file contains all the binary log files in use currently. Screenshot of contents of a binary log index file is provided below. The binary log index below contains 3 binary log files.

```
[root@ip-72-167-246-49 mysql]# cat mysql-bin.index
/var/lib/mysql/mysql-bin.000003
/var/lib/mysql/mysql-bin.000004
/var/lib/mysql/mysql-bin.000005
```

Screen-shot 5—5: Output of cat command on binary log index

## 5.5   binary log

Binary log is a file that contains events corresponding to data definition language (DDL); such as table creation and data manipulation language (DML) such as, insert, update, delete applied to any database in the server. Binary log is useful in replicating the events to a replica. A screenshot of the contents of the binary log read through mysqlbinlog command is provided below.

```
/*!*/;
# at 5165
#140511   6:56:59 server id 2   end_log_pos 5266   Query     thread_id=353     exec_tim
e=0      error_code=0
SET TIMESTAMP=1399816619/*!*/;
insert into test_break_repl values (4)
/*!*/;
# at 5266
#140511   6:57:27 server id 2   end_log_pos 5367   Query     thread_id=353     exec_tim
e=0      error_code=0
SET TIMESTAMP=1399816647/*!*/;
insert into test_break_repl values (5)
/*!*/;
# at 5367
#140512   5:35:57 server id 2   end_log_pos 5386   Stop
DELIMITER ;
# End of log file
ROLLBACK /* added by mysqlbinlog */;
/*!50003 SET COMPLETION_TYPE=@OLD_COMPLETION_TYPE*/;
[root@ip-72-167-246-49 mysql]#
```

**Screen-shot 5—6: Excerpt from mysqlbinlog run on a binary log file**

## 5.6   relay log index

This file contains a roster of the current relay log files in use on the slave. This is a similar to binary log index file. A screenshot of a relay log index file is presented below.

```
[root@ip-72-167-246-49 mysql]# cat mysqld-relay-bin.index
/var/lib/mysql/mysqld-relay-bin.000004
```

**Screen-shot 5—7: Contents of relay log index file**

## 5.7   relay logs

Relay log files are data files that contain events from the master's binary log.

## 5.8   master.info

This file contains master replication user credential for the slave and the master binary log information when change master command is issued on the slave to establish replication.

```
[root@ip-72-167-246-49 mysql]# cat master.info
14
mysql-bin.000007
2363
mobilestatisticsprofessor.us
repl
velcro20
3306
60
0
```

Screen-shot 5—8: Contents of master.info file

## 5.9  relay-log.info

This file contains slave's relay log file and position Slave SQL thread has executed to and the last read master binary log file and position Slave I/O has read to. A screenshot of a relay-log.info is presented below.

```
/var/lib/mysql/mysqld-relay-bin.000004
243
mysql-bin.000007
2363
```

Screen-shot 5—9: Contents of relay-log.info file

## 5.10  Replication Threads

Three threads run in master and slave to facilitate replication.

### 5.10.1  Binlog dump

This thread run in the master in response to slave connecting to the master for the first time after *start slave* is executed on slave successfully. This thread reads master's binary log and supplies log events to slave's I/O thread.

### 5.10.2  Slave I/O

This thread runs on slave when *start slave* command is executed successfully on slave. This thread reads master's binary log events in cooperation with master's Binlog dump thread and write's slave's relay log bin.

### 5.10.3  Slave SQL

This thread runs on slave when *start slave* command is executed successfully on slave. This thread reads slave's relay log bin and applies log events to the slave's databases.

### 5.11  Summary

This chapter presented the replication system components comprising of file system and processes.

# 6   Approach to establish MySQL Replication

This chapter presents high-level approach to establish replication.

**Copy master to replica** – In order for master to replicate to a slave, copy identified master databases to the slave. By doing so, the master and slave will contain the same data. Chapter 7 describes how to copy master to a replica.

**Make configuration file changes** – Master needs to be running on binary logging mode. Master and slave needs to have unique server id. In addition, master and slave may set auto_increment *increment* and *auto_increment_offset* variables to generate unique auto_increment values. My.cnf file needs to be changed to reflect appropriate setting. Chapter 8 describes how to make configuration file changes.

**Create replication user account** – Replication user account needs to be created in the master to allow slave to read master's binary log. If a master is replicating to multiple slaves, multiple replication user accounts need to be created in the master to allow replication user from each slave to connect to the master. Chapter 10 presents how to set up replication user account for various replication topologies.

**Restart the server** – Master and slave need to be restarted after configuration changes are made.

**Record master's binary log coordinates** – Execute show master command on master and record binary log file name and position. Slaves to establish replication will use these.

**Execute change master command on slave** – Execute this command to instruct slave to replicate from master.

**Start slave** – Execute this command on slave to start slave.

**Show slave status** – Execute this command on slave to verify that slave processes are running.

**Show processlist** – Execute this command on master and slave to check processes running to counter verify that replication is running successfully.


Chapter 9 presents useful commands to start replication and to monitor replication.

Chapter 11-16 presents how to establish replication using various replication configurations.

# 7 Copying master databases to replica

Three options available to copy master databases to replica are logical backup using mysqldump, data export & import using infile & output file option in MySQL session and file system copy. MySQL provides a utility called *mysqldump* to copy databases and tables. This utility creates DDL to create database objects and DML to populate the database objects. The other option available is to make a copy of the file system from master to slave. File system can be copied directly from master to slave. However, this process can require disk storage space and time to transfer and copy data. As an alternative, if the OS supports LVM, then LVM snapshot can be created on the master and the slave can synch the lvm. This is the fastest way to copy the master to slave.

## 7.1 Copying using mysqldump

The built in utility mysqldump offers a logical backup of master. The output of mysqldump is human readable DDL and DML. The output can be saved in the master and transferred to the slave and applied on the slave. Alternatively, the output of mysqldump can be piped to the slave to be applied simultaneously thus bypass intermediate storage requirement.

The mysqldump options useful for creating replica of master are presented in the table below.

| Option | Action | Limitation |
| --- | --- | --- |
| --master-data | • Master data implicitly turns off lock-tables and applies lock-all-tables unless single-transaction is specified.<br>• This option records log file name and log file position at the beginning of the mysqldump and issues change master to statement at the beginning of the dump file for the slave to start replicating. However, lave will not replicate until start slave command is issued in the slave. | |
| --single-transaction | • This is similar to a checkpoint. This option makes mysqldump to issue begin transaction before starting to dump data. After the issuance of this | Master data and single transaction can be used in the same command |

| Option | Action | Limitation |
|---|---|---|
|  | statement, any data changes recorded in the log will not be reflected in the mysqldump output |  |
| --lock-all-tables | This option locks all tables across all the databases at the beginning of mysqldump. | This option can not be used in conjunction with single_transaction option |
| --lock-tables | This option locks each table before the table is dumped. | Can not be used with master-data or single-transaction or lock-all-tables option |
| --lock-tables=false | Allows writes to occur on source table. This is can be used if transactions are allowed. |  |
| --all-databases | Dump all databases |  |
| --databases | To specify multiple databases to dump |  |
| --add-drop-database | Add drop database statement before the issuance of create database. The default action of mysqldump without specifying this option is to issue create database statement. |  |
| --skip-add-lock | This option causes lock table statement not to be added before each table insert. |  |

Table 7—1: mysqldump options

## 7.2   Various mysqldump options

This section presents various ways to backup and create a replica of the master using mysqldump.

### 7.2.1   Flush tables with read lock option

Using this option, obtain a global read lock on the entire server across all the databases. Then, run mysqldump to copy the data from master. Once data is copied, apply the data to the replica. Or, apply to the replica simultaneously piping the data through the network. Once copying to replica completes, unlock tables on master. This is the best mysqldump option.

| Srl. No | Actions | Master | Replica |
|---|---|---|---|
| 1 | • Place master server in global read only mode in a MySQL session. Keep the session on to issue unlock tables in step 4 | flush tables with read lock | |
| 2 | • Dump all databases from source and re-direct the output to a data file. <br> • Copy the dump file to target <br> • Execute SQL statements from mysqldump file in the target | mysqldump --all-databases –h*source_host* –u*source_user* –p*source_password* > source_mysqldump.sql | mysql –u*target_user* –p*target_password* –h*target_host* < source_mysqldump.sql |
| 3 | • As an alternative to step 3, pipe the mysqldump across the network to the target. This can save costly space both on the source and target. <br> • This can save costly space both on the source and target. | Mysqldump -u*source_user* –p*source_password* –h*source_host* –all-databases \| mysql –u*target_user* –h*target_host* –p*target_password* | |
| 4 | • Unlock read only mode in the same session as in step 1 | unlock tables | |
| 5 | • Identify the log file name and log file position from the master in a mysql session on the source or master <br> • Issue change master on slave to point to master to replicate from | show master status | change master to |

Table 7—2: Flush tables with read lock mysqldump option

## 7.2.2 master data option

This option writes master's log coordinates to the output, write DDL, implicitly applies locks tables, writes data and unlocks tables. After data is copied, slave can be started without issuing change master command on slave.

| Srl. No | Actions | Master | Replica |
|---|---|---|---|
| 1 | • Dump all databases from source and re-direct the output to a data file.<br>• Copy the dump file to target<br>• Execute SQL statements from mysqldump file in the target | mysqldump --all-databases –master-data –h*source_host* – u*source_user* – p*source_password* > source_mysqldump.sql | mysql –u*target_user* – p*target_password* – h*target_host* < source_mysqldump.sql |
| 2 | • As an alternative to step 1, pipe the mysqldump across the network to the target. This can save costly space both on the source and target. | Mysqldump - u*source_user* – p*source_password* – h*source_host* –master-data –all-databases \| mysql –u*target_user* – h*target_host* – p*target_password* | Alternatively, the process can be started in the slave server.<br><br>Mysqldump - u*source_user* – p*source_password* – h*source_host* –master-data –all-databases \| mysql –u*target_user* – h*target_host* – p*target_password* |

Table 7—3: mysqldump –master-data option

An excerpt of the mysqldump output file using master data option is shown below.

```
CHANGE MASTER TO MASTER_LOG_FILE='mysql-bin.000005', MASTER_LOG_POS=1248;
```

**Screen-shot 7—1: Excerpt from SQL file generated by mysqldump**

An excerpt of the mysqldump output file showing database creation is shown below.

```
CREATE DATABASE /*!32312 IF NOT EXISTS*/ `altmanzscore` /*!40100 DEFAULT CHARACTER SET latin1 */;

USE `altmanzscore`;
```

**Screen-shot 7—2: Excerpt from SQL file generated by mysqldump showing database creation**

An excerpt of the mysqldump output file showing table locking, writing and table unlocking operation is shown below.

```
LOCK TABLES `login` WRITE;
INSERT INTO `login` VALUES (...);
UNLOCK TABLES;
```

**Screen-shot 7—3: Except from SQL file generated by mysqldump displaying lock table and unlock table statements**

### 7.2.3 Single transaction option

If the data up to the point of execution of mysqldump command is required in the slave and the slave can forgo the transactions taken place in the master after the commencement of mysqldump, then single transaction option is desirable. This option creates the effect of a checkpoint and copies transactions up to that checkpoint and ignore transactions after the checkpoint.

| Srl. No | Actions | Master | Replica |
|---|---|---|---|
| 1 | • Dump all databases from source and re-direct the output to a data file.<br>• Copy the dump file to target<br>• Execute SQL statements from mysqldump file in the target | mysqldump --all-databases –single-transaction –h*source_host* –u*source_user* –p*source_password* > source_mysqldump.sql | mysql –u*target_user* –p*target_password* –h*target_host* < source_mysqldump.sql |
| 2 | • As an alternative to step 3, pipe the mysqldump across the network to the target in a mysql session on the target or slave. | Mysqldump --single-transaction –u*source_user* –p*source_password* –h*source_host* –all-databases \| mysql –u*target_user* –h*target_host* –p*target_password* | Alternatively, the process can be started on the target.<br><br>Mysqldump --single-transaction –u*source_user* –p*source_password* –h*source_host* –all-databases \| mysql –u*target_user* –h*target_host* –p*target_password* |
| 3 | • Identify the log file name and log file position from the master in a mysql session<br>• Issue change master on slave to point to master to replicate from in a mysql session | show master status | change master to |

Table 7—4: mysqldump –single-transaction option

### 7.2.4  Lock-all-tables option

Depending on the requirement, lock-all-tables can lock all tables across the database before dumping the tables.

| Srl. No | Actions | Master | Replica |
|---|---|---|---|
| 1 | • Dump all databases from source and re-direct the output to a data file.<br>• Copy the dump file to target<br>• Execute SQL statements from mysqldump file in the target | mysqldump --all-databases –lock-all-tables –h*source_host* –u*source_user* –p*source_password* > source_mysqldump.sql<br><br>mysql –u*target_user* –p*target_password* –h*target_host* < source_mysqldump.sql | Alternately, the process can be run on the target.<br><br>Mysqldump --all-databases –lock-all-tables –h*source_host* –u*source_user* –p*source_password* > source_mysqldump.sql<br><br>mysql –u*target_user* –p*target_password* –h*target_host* < source_mysqldump.sql |
| 2 | • As an alternative to step 3, pipe the mysqldump across the network to the target. This can save costly space both on the source and target. | Mysqldump --lock-all-tables –u*source_user* –p*source_password* –h*source_host* –all-databases \| mysql –u*target_user* –h*target_host* –p*target_password* | |
| 3 | • Identify the log file name and log file position from the master in a mysql session<br>• Issue change master on slave to point to master to replicate from in a mysql session | show master status | change master to |

Table 7—5: mysqldump –lock-all-tables option

## 7.2.5   Lock-tables option

Depending on the requirement, lock-tables can lock tables before dumping the table and unlock the table after dumping the table.

| Srl. No | Actions | Master | Replica |
|---|---|---|---|
| 1 | • Dump all databases from source and re-direct the output to a data file.<br>• Copy the dump file to target<br>• Execute SQL statements from mysqldump file in the target | mysqldump --all-databases --tables –h*source_host* –u*source_user* –p*source_password* > source_mysqldump.sql | mysql –u*target_user* –p*target_password* –h*target_host* < source_mysqldump.sql |
| 2 | • As an alternative to step 3, pipe the mysqldump across the network to the target. This can save costly space both on the source and target. | Mysqldump --lock-tables –u*source_user* –p*source_password* –h*source_host* –all-databases \| mysql –u*target_user* –h*target_host* –p*target_password* | Alternatively, the process can be run entirely in the target.<br><br>Mysqldump --lock-tables –u*source_user* –p*source_password* –h*source_host* –all-databases \| mysql –u*target_user* –h*target_host* –p*target_password* |
| 3 | • Identify the log file name and log file position from the master in a mysql session<br>• Issue change master on slave to point to master to replicate from in a mysql session | show master status | change master to |

Table 7—6: mysqldump –lock-tables option

### 7.2.6   Option to dump a single database

Instead of all databases, a single database can be dumped. In place of –all-databases, substitute the database name

### 7.2.7   Loading to target without binary logging

In case space is limited for faster execution of mysqldump SQL file is desired, binary logging can be turned off on the target.

#### *7.2.7.1   To turn off binary logging:*

1.  Check whether binary logging is turned on

```
mysql> show variables like 'log_bin';
+---------------+-------+
| Variable_name | Value |
+---------------+-------+
| log_bin       | ON    |
+---------------+-------+
1 row in set (0.00 sec)
```

**Screen-shot 7—4: Result of executing show variable command to check the status of binary logging**

2.  In my.cnf file comment out the log_bin statement by adding a # at the beginning.

```
#log_bin=/var/lib/mysql/mysql-bin.log
```

**Screen-shot 7—5: Excerpt of my.cnf displaying commented out log_bin line**

3.  Then, re-start the server.

```
[root@mob ~]# /etc/init.d/mysqld restart
Stopping MySQL:                                            [  OK  ]
Starting MySQL:                                            [  OK  ]
```

**Screen-shot 7—6: Output of MySQL restart command executed in Linux command prompt**

4.  Check binary logging status again

```
mysql> show variables like 'log_bin';
+---------------+-------+
| Variable_name | Value |
+---------------+-------+
| log_bin       | OFF   |
+---------------+-------+
1 row in set (0.00 sec)
```

**Screen-shot 7—7: Result of executing show variables command to check the status of binary logging**

After server is restarted, attempt to run SQL statements from the mysqldump session. Or, start mysql dump and pipe the data over to the target mysql server.

### 7.2.7.2  To turn binary logging on

1. In my.cnf file remove the # in front of log_bin line
2. Then, re-start the server.

## 7.3  Exporting data using outfile and importing data using LOAD DATA INFILE

Data can be copied from a table by using select...outfile option where field and record terminators can be specified. The output file can be loaded to the replica by using LOAD DATA. This can save space compared to mysqldump.

Examples of select ... outfile and load data are presented below.

### 7.3.1  Export data using select...outfile

Data is selected from a table into a data file with specified field and record separator. The file size generated using this option is smaller compared to the one generated using mysqldump.

```
mysql> select * into outfile '/tmp/infile_test.txt'  FIELDS TERMINATED BY ',' OP
TIONALLY ENCLOSED by '"' LINES TERMINATED BY '\n' FROM  test_mysqldump;
Query OK, 1 row affected (0.01 sec)
```

**Screen-shot 7—8: Select data into OUTFILE**

### 7.3.2  Import data using LOAD DATA INFILE command

Data file can be loaded to a table efficiently using LOAD DATA INFILE command. This is an efficient way to load data to a table from a file.

```
mysql> LOAD DATA INFILE '/tmp/infile_test.txt'  INTO TABLE test_mysqldump FIELDS
 TERMINATED BY ',' OPTIONALLY ENCLOSED by '"' LINES TERMINATED BY '\n';
Query OK, 1 row affected (0.02 sec)
Records: 1  Deleted: 0  Skipped: 0  Warnings: 0
```

**Screen-shot 7—9: Example of LOAD DATA INFILE**

## 7.4   File system copy

Data file from master can be copied to replica. This requires the master to be shutdown for
the duration of the copy operation to maintain data consistency between master and
replica. Two options are available to make such copy – LVM (Logical Volume Manager) and
direct copying of master's file system data directory. The master's file system can be copied
across the network, archive can be created using tar and written to tape and then copied to
the replica.

| Method | Actions on Source | Actions on Target |
|---|---|---|
| LVM | Flush tables with read lock | |
| | Create lvm snapshot | Stop mysql server Synch lvm to the replica using rsynch Start MySQL server |
| | Unlock tables Remove the lvm copy | |
| Cold copy | Stop MySQL server | Stop MySQL server |
| | | Copy MySQL data directory from source |
| | Start MySQL server | Start MySQL server |

**Table 7—7: File system copy options to replicate replica from master**

## 7.5   Summary

This chapter presented ways to copy master to replica. Mysqldump,
SELECT..OUTFILE/LOAD DATA INFILE, file system copy and LVM. LVM is most efficient if
the OS supports of all copying methods including mysqldump. Mysqldump is inefficient
space and time wise, but is simpler to carry out copying using mysqldump.

# 8   Changing my.cnf configuration file to support replication

MySQL starts up parameters are specified in my.cnf file. Many options can be specified in this file. The replication related options are presented here. Minimum and expanded configuration parameters for multiple replication configurations are presented which can be readily adopted into my.cnf to establish replication.

Server id variable *server_id* needs to assume a unique integer value within the replication topology. Auto_increment_increment can assume a value the same as the number of master servers in a replication configuration + 1. Auto_increment_offset can assume a value between 1 and the number of master servers in the replication configuration. Binary logging must be turned on in the master server via *log_bin* parameter. A master server can become passive by starting in "read only" mode by specifying *read_only=1* in the configuration file.  A slave server can replicate from master in "read only" mode by specifying *read_only=1* in the configuration file. In case a slave is replicating to another slave, then the master slave needs to log slave updates by setting *log_slave_updates* and run on binary logging mode by setting *log_bin*. Both these parameters need to be set up in the replicating slave.

Useful my.cnf configuration parameters are presented in table 8.1.

| Srl. No. | Parameter | Required or optional | Purpose |
|---|---|---|---|
| 1 | server_id | Required | Server participating in replication topology need to have a unique server id. |
| 2 | log_bin | • Mandatory for master<br>• Mandatory for a slave serving as a master for another slave | For the server to log transactional events in binary log file.<br><br>Log file location and file name format can be specified after equal sign. |
| 3 | relay_log | Optional, but good practice to specify the file format and location | Relay log file location and file name format can be specified after equal sign. |
| 4 | log_slave_updates | Required for a slave serving as a master for another slave | Chaining of slaves to replicate one slave to the other starting from the master. |

| Srl. No. | Parameter | Required or optional | Purpose |
| --- | --- | --- | --- |
| 5 | read_only | Optional, but good practice to specify for the passive master and slave configuration Required for a slave | Passive master and slaves should be in read only mode to avoid data getting out of synch with the master. |
| 6 | auto_increment_increment | Optional, but a good practice for master-master configuration | In Master-master or master-slave configurations, to avoid collision of key values populated through auto increment. |
| 7 | auto_increment_off_set | Optional, but good practice for master-master configuration | In Master-master and master-slave configurations, to avoid collision of key values populated through auto increment. |
| 8 | slave_skip_errors | Optional | This option allows slave to skip specified SQL errors. More than one SQL error number can be specified separated by comma. |
| 9 | replicate_do_db | Optional | Which database(s) to replicate. If more than one database needs to be replicated, then specify them in one line at a time. |
| 10 | replicate_ignore_db | Optional | Which database(s) not to be replicated. If more than one database needs to be replicated, then specify them in one line at a time. |
| 11 | replicate_do_table | Optional | Which database table(s) to replicate. |

| Srl. No. | Parameter | Required or optional | Purpose |
| --- | --- | --- | --- |
| | | | If more than one table needs to be replicated, then specify them in one line at a time. Table names need to appear as database name.table name convention. |
| 12 | replicate_ignore_table | Optional | Which database table(s) not to be replicated. If more than one table needs to be skipped then specify them in one line at a time. Table names need to appear as database name.table name convention. |
| 13 | sql_slave_skip_counter | Optional | How many events should the slave skip from master? This is used to solve SQL Errors. |

**Table 8—1: MySQL configuration file my.cnf related to replication**

Examples of minimum and expanded my.cnf configurations for various master-slave replication topologies are presented table 8.2 and 8.3. Server id can be selected by the DBA, but needs to be unique in the replication topology. Expire_logs_days need to be set up to support organization's recovery point objectives.

| Configu ration | Master | Master | Master | Slave | Slave |
|---|---|---|---|---|---|
| Master-Master Active-Active | server_id=1<br><br>log_bin | server_id=2<br><br>log_bin | | | |
| Master-Master Active-Passive | server_id=1<br><br>log_bin | server_id=2<br><br>log_bin<br><br>read_only=1 | | | |
| Master-Master-Master Circular | server_id=1<br><br>log_bin | server_id=2<br><br>log_bin | server_id=3<br><br>log_bin | | |
| Master-Slave | server_id=1<br><br>log_bin | | | server_id=2 | |
| Master-Slave - Slave<br><br>Chain | server_id=1<br><br>log_bin | | | server_id=2<br><br>Log_bin<br><br>Log_slave_updates | server_id=3 |
| Master-Master Active-Active + 2 Slaves | server_id=1<br><br>log_bin | server_id=2<br><br>log_bin | | server_id=3 | server_id=4 |

**Table 8—2: Minimum configuration parameters need to be added to my.cnf file to establish replication**

| Configu ration | Master | Master | Master | Slave | Slave |
|---|---|---|---|---|---|
| Master-Master Active-Active | server_id=1<br><br>log_bin=/var/ lib/mysql/my | server_id=2<br><br>log_bin=/va r/lib/mysql | | | |

| Configuration | Master | Master | Master | Slave | Slave |
|---|---|---|---|---|---|
| | sql-bin.log<br><br>relay_log=/var/lib/mysql/mysqld-relay-bin.log<br><br>expire_logs_days=1<br><br>auto_increment_increment=3<br><br>auto_increment_offset=1 | /mysql-bin.log<br><br>relay_log=/var/lib/mysql/mysqld-relay-bin.log<br><br>expire_logs_days=1<br><br>auto_increment_increment=3<br><br>auto_increment_offset=2 | | | |
| Master-Master Active-Passive | server_id=1<br><br>log_bin=/var/lib/mysql/mysql-bin.log<br><br>relay_log=/var/lib/mysql/mysqld-relay-bin.log<br><br>expire_logs_days=1<br><br>auto_increment_increment=3<br>auto_increment_offset=1 | server_id=2<br><br>log_bin=/var/lib/mysql/mysql-bin.log<br><br>relay_log=/var/lib/mysql/mysqld-relay-bin.log<br><br>expire_logs_days=1<br><br>auto_increment_increment=3<br><br>auto_increment_offset=2<br><br>read_only= | | | |

| Configu ration | Master | Master | Master | Slave | Slave |
|---|---|---|---|---|---|
| | | 1 | | | |
| Master-Master-Master circular | server_id=1<br>log_bin=/var/lib/mysql/mysql-bin.log<br><br>relay_log=/var/lib/mysql/mysqld-relay-bin.log<br><br>expire_logs_days=1<br><br>auto_increment_increment=4<br><br>auto_increment_offset=1 | server_id=2<br>log_bin=/var/lib/mysql/mysql-bin.log<br><br>relay_log=/var/lib/mysql/mysqld-relay-bin.log<br><br>expire_logs_days=1<br><br>auto_increment_increment=4<br><br>auto_increment_offset=2 | server_id=3<br>log_bin=/var/lib/mysql/mysql-bin.log<br><br>relay_log=/var/lib/mysql/mysqld-relay-bin.log<br><br>expire_logs_days=1<br><br>auto_increment_increment=4<br><br>auto_increment_offset=3 | | |
| Master-Slave | server_id=1<br><br>log_bin=/var/lib/mysql/mysql-bin.log<br>relay_log=/var/lib/mysql/mysqld-relay-bin.log<br><br>expire_logs_days=1<br><br>auto_increment_increment=3 | | | Server_id=2<br><br>relay_log=/var/lib/mysql/mysqld-relay-bin.log<br><br>auto_increment_increment=3<br><br>auto_in | |

| Configuration | Master | Master | Master | Slave | Slave |
| --- | --- | --- | --- | --- | --- |
| | auto_increment_offset=1 | | | crement_offset=2 | |
| Master-Slave – Slave<br><br>Chain | server_id=1<br><br>log_bin=/var/lib/mysql/mysql-bin.log<br><br>relay_log=/var/lib/mysql/mysqld-relay-bin.log<br><br>expire_logs_days=1<br><br>auto_increment_increment=4<br><br>auto_increment_offset=1 | | | server_id=2<br><br>log_bin=/var/lib/mysql/mysql-bin.log<br><br>relay_log=/var/lib/mysql/mysqld-relay-bin.log<br><br>expire_logs_days=1<br><br>Log_slave_updates<br><br>auto_increment_increment=4<br><br>auto_increment_offset=2 | server_id=3<br><br>relay_log=/var/lib/mysql/mysqld-relay-bin.log<br><br>auto_increment_increment=4<br><br>auto_increment_offset=3 |
| Master and 2 Slaves | server_id=1<br><br>log_bin=/var/lib/mysql/mysql-bin.log | | | server_id=2<br><br>relay_log=/var/lib/mys | server_id=3<br><br>relay_log=/var/lib/mysql/ |

| Configuration | Master | Master | Master | Slave | Slave |
|---|---|---|---|---|---|
| | relay_log=/var/lib/mysql/mysqld-relay-bin.log<br><br>expire_logs_days=1<br><br>auto_increment_increment=4<br>auto_increment_offset=1 | | | ql/mysqld-relay-bin.log<br><br>auto_increment_increment=4<br><br>auto_increment_offset=2 | mysqld-relay-bin.log auto_increment_increment=4<br><br>auto_increment_offset=3 |
| Master-Master Active-Active<br><br>+<br><br>Each master has its own slave | server_id=1<br><br>log_bin=/var/lib/mysql/mysql-bin.log<br><br>relay_log=/var/lib/mysql/mysqld-relay-bin.log<br><br>expire_logs_days=1<br><br>auto_increment_increment=5<br><br>auto_increment_offset=1 | server_id=2<br><br>log_bin=/var/lib/mysql/mysql-bin.log<br>relay_log=/var/lib/mysql/mysqld-relay-bin.log<br><br>expire_logs_days=1<br><br>auto_increment_increment=5<br><br>auto_increment_offset=2 | | server_id=3<br><br>relay_log=/var/lib/mysql/mysqld-relay-bin.log<br><br>auto_increment_increment=5<br><br>auto_increment_offset=3 | server_id=4<br><br>relay_log=/var/lib/mysql/mysqld-relay-bin.log auto_increment_increment=5<br><br>auto_increment_offset=4 |

Table 8—3: Expanded configuration parameters to be added to my.cnf file to establish replication

## 8.1 Summary

This chapter presented my.cnf configuration parameters to be used with a variety of master-slave configurations.

# 9  Commands to establish and monitor replication

A set of commands that are useful to establish replication, to monitor replication status and threads are presented in this chapter. A roster of MySQL and OS level commands useful for replication is presented here.

| Srl. No. | Command | Purpose |
|---|---|---|
| 1 | show master status | To display the master log coordinates – master log file name and log file position. |
| 2 | show slave status | To display the status of the slave. |
| 3 | start slave | To start slave. |
| 4 | stop slave | To stop slave. |
| 5 | reset slave | To make slave to forget about master coordinates. |
| 6 | reset master | To clear master binary log index file, but does not delete the binary log files. |
| 7 | show global variables like 'log_bin' | To display whether the server is running in binary logging mode. |
| 8 | show global variables like 'server_id' | To display server id variable |
| 9 | show global variables like 'auto_increment_increment' | To display values of auto_increment_increment variable |
| 10 | show global variables like 'auto_increment_offset' | To display values of auto_increment_offset variable |
| 11 | show binary logs | To display list of binary log files in use currently. |
| 12 | show processlist | To display threads running on the server. |
| 13 | grant | To grant privileges to a user |
| 14 | show grants for user | To display privileges granted to a user |
| 15 | show status like 'slave_running' | To display whether slave is running |
| 16 | flush privileges | To make recently changed privileges to become effective |
| 17 | show slave hosts | To display all the slave hosts connected to the master |
| 18 | flush logs | Closes all open logs and re-opens new log files. This command does not delete binary log files. |
| 19 | flush tables with read lock | Places the server in global read only mode. |

| Srl. No. | Command | Purpose |
| --- | --- | --- |
| 20 | unlock tables | Releases global read only mode |
| 21 | change master to master_host=<master host>, master_user=<master user>, master_password=<master password>, master_log_file=<master log_file>, master_log_pos=<position> | To make slave to start replicating from a master. This only updates master.info, but does not start the slave processes until the slave is started via start slave command, |
| 22 | /etc/init.d/mysqld stop | Stop MySQL Server |
| 23 | /etc/init.d/mysqld start | Start MySQL Server |
| 24 | /etc/init.d/mysqld restart | Re-start MySQL Server |
| 25 | mysqlbinlog | Read events from binary log and relay-log files. |
| 26 | Purge binary logs | This command deletes binary log files. |

Table 9—1: Commands to establish and monitor replication


## 9.1 Summary

This chapter presented a list of useful commands to use while starting or monitoring MySQL replication.

# 10 Creating Replication User Account

Replication user needs to be created in master to allow connection from slave to read the master's binary log. Replication user must be granted *replication slave* privilege on master. This privilege enables the I/O thread running on slave to read binary log from the master using the replication credentials. Optionally, *replication client* privilege can be granted to the replication user on master. This privilege allows show master status and show slave status type of commands to be executed.

If a master allows multiple slaves to connect, then multiple replication accounts need to be created in the master.

## 10.1 Replication Privileges

Replication slave privilege is critical to the replication operation. Replication client privilege is optional.

**Replication Slave** – This privilege allows replication user to read binary log of the master. This is the <u>minimum</u> privilege the replication user must have to read the master's binary log.

**Replication Client** – This privilege allows to execute show master status and show slave status type of commands. This is an optional privilege for the replication user.

## 10.2 Replication slave host

Replication user needs to be created in the master MySQL server to allow the slave to connect to. Correct host information must be supplied to allow replication user to read master's binary log.

## 10.3 How to create the replication user

Creating user and granting privileges can be accomplished by one of the following two ways – either via grant command or via create user and grant commands.

Example of the user creation is as follows.  Here, the replication host is mobilestatisticsprofessor.us. Replication user id is *repl*. Replication user password is *velcro20*. The choice of user id and password is up to the DBA as long as the values are permissible within MySQL.

*grant replication slave, replication client on *.* to 'repl'@'mobilestatisticsprofessor.us' identified by 'velcro20';*

OR

*create user 'repl'@'mobilestatisticsprofessor.us' identified by 'velcro20';*

*grant replication slave, replication client on *.* to 'repl'@'mobilestatisticsprofessor.us'*

After user is created, optionally *flush privileges* command is issued.  This allows the privileges to be effective immediately.

The following diagram illustrates 7 master-slave configurations and replication user set up. Mobilestatisticsprofessor.com, mobilestatisticsprofessor.us, mobilestatisticsprofessor.net and mobilestatisticsprofessor.biz are 4 MySQL Servers used in the example. Replication user name is *repl*. Replication user password is *velcro20*.

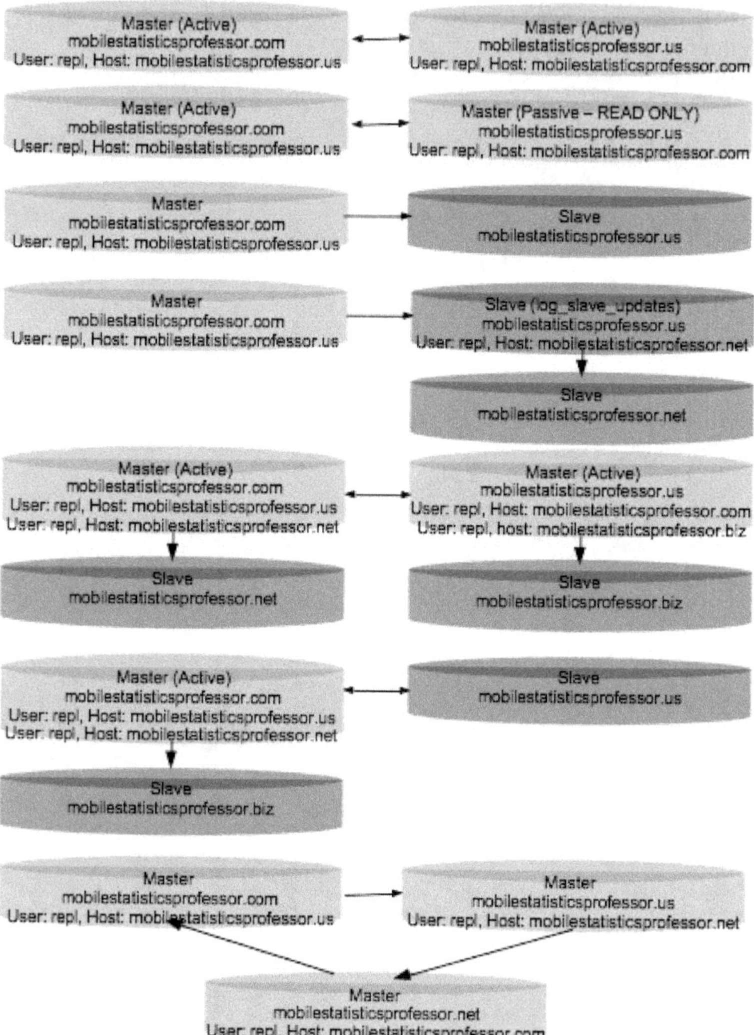


**Figure 10—1: Example of creating user accounts for various replication configurations**

The following table provides commands used in 7 master-slave configurations and replication to set up users. Mobilestatisticsprofessor.com, mobilestatisticsprofessor.us, mobilestatisticsprofessor.net and mobilestatisticsprofessor.biz are 4 MySQL Servers used in the example. Replication user name is *repl*. Replication user password is *velcro20*.

| Replication Configuration | Replication User Accounts |
|---|---|
| Master - Master | <u>Master Host:</u> mobilestatisticsprofessor.com<br><br><u>Master Host:</u> mobilestatisticsprofesor.us<br><br>On mobilestatisticsprofessor.com, create replication user account for mobilestatisticsprofessr.us to read log.<br><br>mysql> grant replication slave, replication client on *.* to 'repl'@'mobilestatisticsprofessor.us' identified by 'velcro20';<br><br>On mobilestatisticsprofessor.us, create replication user account for mobilestatisticsprofessr.com to read log.<br><br>mysql> grant replication slave, replication client on *.* to 'repl'@'mobilestatisticsprofessor.com' identified by 'velcro20'; |
| Master – Slave | <u>Master Host:</u> mobilestatisticsprofessor.com<br><br><u>Slave Host:</u> mobilestatisticsprofesor.us<br><br>On mobilestatisticsprofessor.com, create replication user account for mobilestatisticsprofessr.us to read log.<br><br>mysql> grant replication slave, replication client on *.* to 'repl'@'mobilestatisticsprofessor.us' identified by 'velcro20'; |

| Replication Configuration | Replication User Accounts |
| --- | --- |
| Master-<br>Slave-<br>Slave | <u>Master Host:</u>  mobilestatisticsprofessor.com<br><br><u>Slave Host:</u> mobilestatisticsprofesor.us<br><br><u>Slave Host:</u> mobilestatisticsprofesor.net<br><br>On mobilestatisticsprofessor.com, create replication user account for mobilestatisticsprofessr.us to read log.<br><br>mysql> grant replication slave, replication client on *.* to 'repl'@'mobilestatisticsprofessor.us' identified by 'velcro20';<br><br>On mobilestatisticsprofessor.us, create replication user account for mobilestatisticsprofessr.net to read log.<br><br>mysql> grant replication slave, replication client on *.* to 'repl'@'mobilestatisticsprofessor.net' identified by 'velcro20'; |
| Master-<br>2 or more<br>slaves | <u>Master Host:</u> mobilestatisticsprofessor.com<br><br><u>Slave Host:</u> mobilestatisticsprofesor.us<br><br><u>Slave Host:</u> mobilestatisticsprofesor.net<br><br>On mobilestatisticsprofessor.com, create replication user account for mobilestatisticsprofessr.us to read log.<br><br>mysql> grant replication slave, replication client on *.* to 'repl'@'mobilestatisticsprofessor.us' identified by 'velcro20';<br><br>On mobilestatisticsprofessor.us, create replication user account for mobilestatisticsprofessr.net to read log.<br><br>mysql> grant replication slave, replication client on *.* to 'repl'@'mobilestatisticsprofessor.net' identified by 'velcro20'; |

| Replication Configuration | Replication User Accounts |
| --- | --- |
| Master-Master and each Master replicates to its own slave | <u>Master Host:</u> mobilestatisticsprofessor.com<br><br><u>Slave Host:</u> mobilestatisticsprofesor.net<br><br><u>Master Host:</u> mobilestatisticsprofesor.us<br><br><u>Slave Host:</u> mobilestatisticsprofesor.biz<br><br>On mobilestatisticsprofessor.com, create replication user account for mobilestatisticsprofessr.us and mobilestatisticsprofessor.net to read log.<br><br>mysql> grant replication slave, replication client on *.* to 'repl'@'mobilestatisticsprofessor.us' identified by 'velcro20';<br>mysql> grant replication slave, replication client on *.* to 'repl'@'mobilestatisticsprofessor.net' identified by 'velcro20';<br><br>On mobilestatisticsprofessor.us, create replication user account for mobilestatisticsprofessr.com and mobilestatisticsprofessor.biz to read log.<br><br>mysql> grant replication slave, replication client on *.* to 'repl'@'mobilestatisticsprofessor.com' identified by 'velcro20';<br>mysql> grant replication slave, replication client on *.* to 'repl'@'mobilestatisticsprofessor.biz' identified by 'velcro20'; |

| Replication Configuration | Replication User Accounts |
|---|---|
| Master-Master-Master | <u>Master Host:</u> mobilestatisticsprofessor.com |
| | <u>Master Host:</u> mobilestatisticsprofesor.us |
| Circular | <u>Master Host:</u> mobilestatisticsprofesor.net |
| | On mobilestatisticsprofessor.com, create replication user account for mobilestatisticsprofessr.us to read log. |
| | mysql> grant replication slave, replication client on *.* to 'repl'@'mobilestatisticsprofessor.us' identified by 'velcro20'; |
| | On mobilestatisticsprofessor.us, create replication user account for mobilestatisticsprofessr.net to read log. |
| | mysql> grant replication slave, replication client on *.* to 'repl'@'mobilestatisticsprofessor.net' identified by 'velcro20'; |
| | On mobilestatisticsprofessor.net create replication user account for mobilestatisticsprofessr.com to read log. |
| | mysql> grant replication slave, replication client on *.* to 'repl'@'mobilestatisticsprofessor.com' identified by 'velcro20'; |

**Table 10—1: Example of SQL statements to create replication user accounts for various configurations.**

## 10.4 Summary

This chapter presented how to create replication user account for various replication configurations. Replication user needs to be created in master to allow slave to establish replication. If multiple slaves are establishing replication from master, a replication user account needs to be created for each slave on the master.

# 11 Establishing Master-Master Active-Active Replication

This chapter presents the steps necessary with examples to establish bi-directional master-master-active-active replication. In this replication configuration, the master becomes the slave of the other. Each master replicates binary log events to the other.

## 11.1 Purpose

The purpose of the master-master-active-active replication is to facilitate failover and load balancing to satisfy high availability requirement.

## 11.2 Approach

The approach to establish master-master-active-active replication is as follows.

- Create replication user account in each master to replicate to the other master
- Make configuration changes in my.cnf file
    - Assign unique server id
    - To turn binary logging on
    - Optionally assign log file name format and location
    - Optionally assign relay log file name format and location
    - Set auto_increment_increment and auto_increment_offset
- Restart MySQL server after configuration changes.
- Record master log file name and log position.
- Issue *change master* command on each master to read log from the other master.
- Start slave on each master
- Verify slave status
- Verify process list

## 11.3 Logical Architecture

The logical architecture of master-master-active-active replication configuration is shown the diagram below.

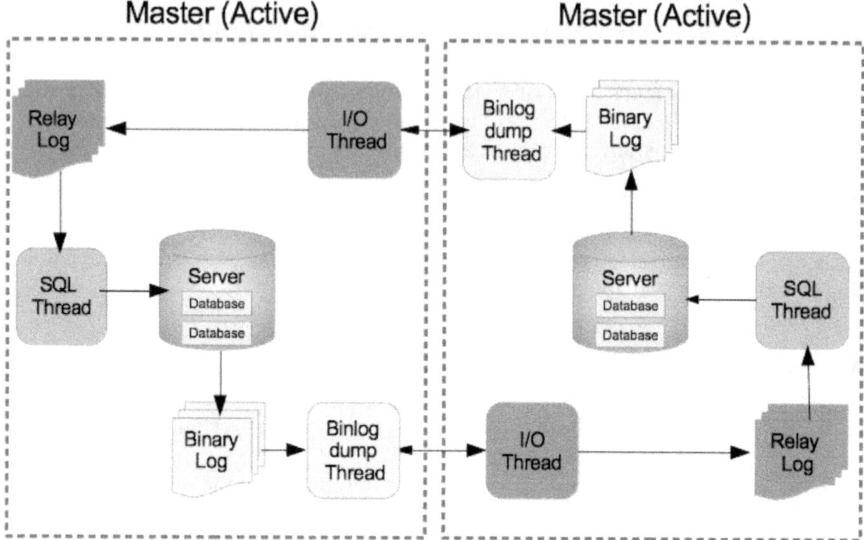

Figure 11—1: Logical Architecture of Master-Master Active-Active Replication Configuration

## 11.4  Physical Architecture

Physical architecture diagram of master-master-active-active replication is shown below.

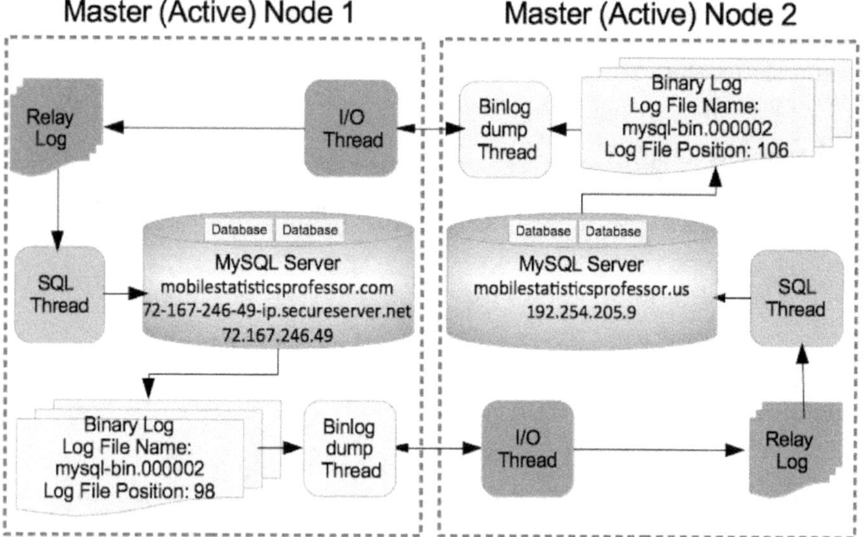

Figure 11—2: Example of Physical Architecture of Master-Master Active-Active Replication Configuration

MySQL server host details are presented in the table below.

| Srl. No. | Node | Host/IP Address | server_id | Role |
|---|---|---|---|---|
| 1 | Node 1 | Mobilestatisticsprofessor.com<br>72-167-246-49-ip.secureserver.net<br>72.167.246.49 | 2 | Node 1 is slave of Node 2 |
| 2 | Node 2 | mobilestatisticsprofessor.us,<br>192.254.205.9 | 1 | Node 2 is slave of Node 1 |

Table 11—1: Master-Master-Active-Active MySQL Server Configuration

## 11.5 Steps

Create replication user account on both Node 1 and Node 2 unless the replication accounts are already created. Create replication user account on Node 1 allowing Node 2 to read logs from Node 1. Similarly, create replication user account on Node 1 allowing Node 2 to read logs from Node 1. Execute *flush privileges* command if necessary. Verify the grans to ensure that the replication user has at least *replication slave* grant. The choice of user id and password is up to the DBA to suit the organization's policies and standards.

Create replication user account on Node 1 allowing Node 2 to read logs from Node 1 and flush privileges.

```
mysql> grant replication slave, replication client on *.* to 'repl'@'mobilestati
sticsprofessor.us' identified by 'velcro20';
Query OK, 0 rows affected (0.00 sec)

mysql> flush privileges;
Query OK, 0 rows affected (0.00 sec)
```

**Screen-shot 11—1: Replication user created in master server Node 1 or mobilestatisticsprofessor.com**

Verify that the replication user created in Node 1 has required privileges to facilitate replication.

```
mysql> show grants for 'repl'@'mobilestatisticsprofessor.us'\G
*************************** 1. row ***************************
Grants for repl@mobilestatisticsprofessor.us: GRANT REPLICATION SLAVE, REPLICATI
ON CLIENT ON *.* TO 'repl'@'mobilestatisticsprofessor.us' IDENTIFIED BY PASSWORD
'5373051f0cfcc009'
1 row in set (0.00 sec)
```

**Screen-shot 11—2: Verifying the replication user account on master mobilestatisticsprofessor.com**

Create replication user account on Node 2 allowing Node 1 to read logs from Node 2 and flush privileges.

```
mysql> grant replication slave, replication client on *.* to 'repl'@'mobilestati
sticsprofessor.com' identified by 'velcro20';
Query OK, 0 rows affected (0.00 sec)

mysql> flush privileges;
Query OK, 0 rows affected (0.00 sec)
```

**Screen-shot 11—3: Added replication user to master mobilestatisticsprofessor.us**

Verify that the replication user created in Node 2 has required privileges to facilitate replication.

```
mysql> show grants for 'repl'@'mobilestatisticsprofessor.com'\G
*************************** 1. row ***************************
Grants for repl@mobilestatisticsprofessor.com: GRANT REPLICATION SLAVE, REPLICAT
ION CLIENT ON *.* TO 'repl'@'mobilestatisticsprofessor.com' IDENTIFIED BY PASSWO
RD '5373051f0cfcc009'
1 row in set (0.00 sec)
```

**Screen-shot 11—4: Verify user grans**

Make necessary configuration changes to the configuration file my.cnf located on Node 1. At a minimum, the following are added unless already present. Auto_increment_increment and auto_increment_offset is set up to avoid collision of auto_increment key values among the MySQL servers participating in the replication configuration. server_id needs to be unique.  These are the minimum parameters, but these can be expanded to suit the particular need of the organization by the DBA.

*bin_log*
*server_id=2*
*auto_increment_increment=3*
*auto_increment_offset=2*

```
[mysqld]
datadir=/var/lib/mysql
socket=/var/lib/mysql/mysql.sock
user=mysql
# Default to using old password format for compatibility with mysql 3.x
# clients (those using the mysqlclient10 compatibility package).
old_passwords=1

#log_bin=/var/lib/mysql/mysql-bin.log
#relay_log=/var/lib/mysql/mysqld-relay-bin.log
#log_slave_updates
server_id=2
expire_logs_days=1
#read_only=1
auto_increment_increment=3
auto_increment_offset=2

[mysqld_safe]
log-error=/var/log/mysqld.log
pid-file=/var/run/mysqld/mysqld.pid
```

**Screen-shot 11—5: Configuration changes in master mobilestatisticsprofessor.com my.cnf file to support replication**

If my.cnf has been modified, restart the MySQL server for the values to take effect.

*$/etc/init.d/mysqld restart*

```
[root@ip-72-167-246-49 ~]# /etc/init.d/mysqld restart
Stopping MySQL:                                            [  OK  ]
Starting MySQL:                                            [  OK  ]
[root@ip-72-167-246-49 ~]#
```

**Screen-shot 11—6: Restarted MySQL server on master mobilestatisticsprofessor.com**

Verify log_bin, auto_increment_increment and auto_increment_offset parameters after the server is restarted to ensure that the parameters have been set correctly in Node 1.

```
mysql> show variables like 'log_bin';
+---------------+-------+
| Variable_name | Value |
+---------------+-------+
| log_bin       | ON    |
+---------------+-------+
1 row in set (0.00 sec)

mysql> show variables like 'server_id';
+---------------+-------+
| Variable_name | Value |
+---------------+-------+
| server_id     | 2     |
+---------------+-------+
1 row in set (0.00 sec)

mysql> show variables like 'auto_increment_increment';
+--------------------------+-------+
| Variable_name            | Value |
+--------------------------+-------+
| auto_increment_increment | 3     |
+--------------------------+-------+
1 row in set (0.00 sec)

mysql> show variables like 'auto_increment_offset';
+-----------------------+-------+
| Variable_name         | Value |
+-----------------------+-------+
| auto_increment_offset | 2     |
+-----------------------+-------+
1 row in set (0.00 sec)
```

**Screen-shot 11—7: Checking the log_bin, server_id, auto_increment_increment and auto_increment_offset variables in master mobilestatisticsprofessor.com**

Make necessary configuration changes to the configuration file my.cnf located on Node 2. At a minimum, the following are added unless already present. Auto_increment_increment and auto_increment_offset is set up to avoid collision of auto_increment key values among the MySQL servers participating in the replication configuration. server_id needs to be unique.  These are the minimum parameters, but these can be expanded to suit the particular need of the organization by the DBA.

*bin_log*
*server_id=2*
*auto_increment_increment=3*
*auto_increment_offset=1*

```
[root@mob ~]# cat /etc/my.cnf
[mysqld]
local-infile=0
max_allowed_packet=16M
set-variable=local-infile=0
datadir=/var/lib/mysql
socket=/var/lib/mysql/mysql.sock
user=mysql
# Default to using old password format for compatibility with mysql 3.x
# clients (those using the mysqlclient10 compatibility package).
old_passwords=1

log_bin=/var/lib/mysql/mysql-bin.log
relay_log=/var/lib/mysql/mysqld-relay-bin.log
server_id=1
expire_logs_days=1
auto_increment_increment=3
auto_increment_offset=1

slave_skip_error=1062

# Disabling symbolic-links is recommended to prevent assorted security risks;
# to do so, uncomment this line:
# symbolic-links=0

#skip-bdb

innodb_buffer_pool_size=2M
innodb_additional_mem_pool_size=500K
innodb_log_buffer_size=500K
innodb_thread_concurrency=2
[mysqld_safe]
log-error=/var/log/mysqld.log
pid-file=/var/run/mysqld/mysqld.pid
#skip-bdb

innodb_buffer_pool_size=2M
innodb_additional_mem_pool_size=500K
innodb_log_buffer_size=500K
innodb_thread_concurrency=2
```

**Screen-shot 11—8: my.cnf changes made in master mobilestatisticsprofessor.us**

If my.cnf has been modified on Node 2, restart the MySQL server for the values to take effect.

*$/etc/init.d/mysqld restart*

```
[root@mob ~]# /etc/init.d/mysqld restart
Stopping MySQL:                                            [  OK  ]
Starting MySQL:                                            [  OK  ]
[root@mob ~]#
```

**Screen-shot 11—9: Restarted MySQL Server on master mobilestatisticsprofessor.us**

Verify log_bin, auto_increment_increment and auto_increment_offset parameters after the server is restarted to ensure that the parameters have been set correctly in Node 2.

```
mysql> show variables like 'log_bin';
+---------------+-------+
| Variable_name | Value |
+---------------+-------+
| log_bin       | ON    |
+---------------+-------+
1 row in set (0.00 sec)

mysql> show variables like 'server_id';
+---------------+-------+
| Variable_name | Value |
+---------------+-------+
| server_id     | 1     |
+---------------+-------+
1 row in set (0.00 sec)

mysql> show variables like 'auto_increment_increment';
+--------------------------+-------+
| Variable_name            | Value |
+--------------------------+-------+
| auto_increment_increment | 3     |
+--------------------------+-------+
1 row in set (0.00 sec)

mysql> show variables like 'auto_increment_offset';
+-----------------------+-------+
| Variable_name         | Value |
+-----------------------+-------+
| auto_increment_offset | 1     |
+-----------------------+-------+
1 row in set (0.00 sec)
```

**Screen-shot 11—10: Checking session variables log_bin, server_id. auto_increment_increment and auto_increment_offset on master mobilestatisticsprofessor.us**

Record log file name and position on Node 1 by executing *show master status* command.

```
[root@ip-72-167-246-49 mysql]# mysql -uroot -p
Enter password:
Welcome to the MySQL monitor.  Commands end with ; or \g.
Your MySQL connection id is 5
Server version: 5.0.77-log Source distribution

Type 'help;' or '\h' for help. Type '\c' to clear the buffer.

mysql> show master status;
+------------------+----------+--------------+------------------+
| File             | Position | Binlog_Do_DB | Binlog_Ignore_DB |
+------------------+----------+--------------+------------------+
| mysql-bin.000002 |       98 |              |                  |
+------------------+----------+--------------+------------------+
1 row in set (0.00 sec)
```

**Screen-shot 11—11: Executed show master status command on master mobilestatisticsprofessor.com**

Similarly, record log file name and position on Node 2 by executing *show master status* command.

```
[root@mob mysql]# mysql -uroot -p
Enter password:
Welcome to the MySQL monitor.  Commands end with ; or \g.
Your MySQL connection id is 207
Server version: 5.1.52-log Source distribution

Copyright (c) 2000, 2010, Oracle and/or its affiliates. All rights reserved.
This software comes with ABSOLUTELY NO WARRANTY. This is free software,
and you are welcome to modify and redistribute it under the GPL v2 license

Type 'help;' or '\h' for help. Type '\c' to clear the current input statement.

mysql> show master status;
+------------------+----------+--------------+------------------+
| File             | Position | Binlog_Do_DB | Binlog_Ignore_DB |
+------------------+----------+--------------+------------------+
| mysql-bin.000002 |      106 |              |                  |
+------------------+----------+--------------+------------------+
1 row in set (0.00 sec)

mysql>
```

**Screen-shot 11—12: Show master status executed on master mobilestatisticsprofessor.us**

Execute *change master* command on Node 1 to establish replication from Node 2. Then, execute *start slave* on Node 1 to start replicating.

```
[root@ip-72-167-246-49 mysql]# mysql -uroot -p
Enter password:
Welcome to the MySQL monitor.  Commands end with ; or \g.
Your MySQL connection id is 7
Server version: 5.0.77-log Source distribution

Type 'help;' or '\h' for help. Type '\c' to clear the buffer.

mysql> change master to master_host='mobilestatisticsprofessor.us', master_user='repl', master_passwo
rd='velcro20', master_log_file='mysql-bin.000002', master_log_pos=106;
Query OK, 0 rows affected (1.36 sec)

mysql>
```

**Screen-shot 11—13: Change master issued on master mobilestatisticsprofessor.com**

Execute *change master* command on Node 2 to establish replication from Node 1. Then, execute *start slave* on Node 2 to start replicating.

```
[root@mob mysql]# mysql -uroot -p
Enter password:
Welcome to the MySQL monitor.  Commands end with ; or \g.
Your MySQL connection id is 318
Server version: 5.1.52-log Source distribution

Copyright (c) 2000, 2010, Oracle and/or its affiliates. All rights reserved.
This software comes with ABSOLUTELY NO WARRANTY. This is free software,
and you are welcome to modify and redistribute it under the GPL v2 license

Type 'help;' or '\h' for help. Type '\c' to clear the current input statement.

mysql> change master to master_host='mobilestatisticsprofessor.com', master_user='repl', master_password='vel
cro20', master_log_file='mysql-bin.000002', master_log_pos=98;
Query OK, 0 rows affected (0.00 sec)
```

**Screen-shot 11—14: Change master command executed on master mobilestatisticsprofessor.us**

Verify slave status on Node 1.  Slave I/O and SQL threads need to run without error for the slave to replicate from master successfully.

```
mysql> show slave status\G
*************************** 1. row ***************************
               Slave_IO_State: Waiting for master to send event
                  Master_Host: mobilestatisticsprofessor.us
                  Master_User: repl
                  Master_Port: 3306
                Connect_Retry: 60
              Master_Log_File: mysql-bin.000002
          Read_Master_Log_Pos: 106
               Relay_Log_File: mysqld-relay-bin.000006
                Relay_Log_Pos: 243
        Relay_Master_Log_File: mysql-bin.000002
             Slave_IO_Running: Yes
            Slave_SQL_Running: Yes
              Replicate_Do_DB:
          Replicate_Ignore_DB:
           Replicate_Do_Table:
       Replicate_Ignore_Table:
      Replicate_Wild_Do_Table:
  Replicate_Wild_Ignore_Table:
                   Last_Errno: 0
                   Last_Error:
                 Skip_Counter: 0
          Exec_Master_Log_Pos: 106
              Relay_Log_Space: 243
              Until_Condition: None
               Until_Log_File:
                Until_Log_Pos: 0
           Master_SSL_Allowed: No
           Master_SSL_CA_File:
           Master_SSL_CA_Path:
              Master_SSL_Cert:
            Master_SSL_Cipher:
               Master_SSL_Key:
        Seconds_Behind_Master: 0
1 row in set (0.00 sec)
```

**Screen-shot 11—15: show slave status command executed on master mobilestatisticsprofessor.com**

Verify slave status on Node 2. Slave I/O and SQL threads need to run without error for the slave to replicate from master successfully.

```
mysql> show slave status\G
*************************** 1. row ***************************
               Slave_IO_State: Waiting for master to send event
                  Master_Host: mobilestatisticsprofessor.com
                  Master_User: repl
                  Master_Port: 3306
                Connect_Retry: 60
              Master_Log_File: mysql-bin.000002
          Read_Master_Log_Pos: 98
               Relay_Log_File: mysqld-relay-bin.000005
                Relay_Log_Pos: 243
        Relay_Master_Log_File: mysql-bin.000002
             Slave_IO_Running: Yes
            Slave_SQL_Running: Yes
              Replicate_Do_DB:
          Replicate_Ignore_DB:
           Replicate_Do_Table:
       Replicate_Ignore_Table:
      Replicate_Wild_Do_Table:
  Replicate_Wild_Ignore_Table:
                   Last_Errno: 0
                   Last_Error:
                 Skip_Counter: 0
          Exec_Master_Log_Pos: 98
              Relay_Log_Space: 536
              Until_Condition: None
               Until_Log_File:
                Until_Log_Pos: 0
           Master_SSL_Allowed: No
           Master_SSL_CA_File:
           Master_SSL_CA_Path:
              Master_SSL_Cert:
            Master_SSL_Cipher:
               Master_SSL_Key:
        Seconds_Behind_Master: 0
Master_SSL_Verify_Server_Cert: No
                Last_IO_Errno: 0
                Last_IO_Error:
               Last_SQL_Errno: 0
               Last_SQL_Error:
1 row in set (0.00 sec)
```

**Screen-shot 11—16: show slave status command executed on master mobilestatistcsprofessor.us**

Verify the processlist on Node 1.  Node 1 has sent all its logs to Node 2 as shown by the *Binlog dump* process id 8. Node 1 has also processed the binary log of its master Node 2 as shown in the process id 10.

```
mysql> show processlist\G
*************************** 1. row ***************************
     Id: 7
   User: root
   Host: localhost
     db: NULL
Command: Query
   Time: 0
  State: NULL
   Info: show processlist
*************************** 2. row ***************************
     Id: 8
   User: repl
   Host: 192.254.205.8:51975
     db: NULL
Command: Binlog Dump
   Time: 76
  State: Has sent all binlog to slave; waiting for binlog to be updated
   Info: NULL
*************************** 3. row ***************************
     Id: 9
   User: system user
   Host:
     db: NULL
Command: Connect
   Time: 69
  State: Waiting for master to send event
   Info: NULL
*************************** 4. row ***************************
     Id: 10
   User: system user
   Host:
     db: NULL
Command: Connect
   Time: 68
  State: Has read all relay log; waiting for the slave I/O thread to update it
   Info: NULL
4 rows in set (0.00 sec)

mysql>
```

**Screen-shot 11—17: Show processlist executed on master mobilestatisticsprofessor.com**

Verify the processlist on Node 2.  Node 2 has sent all its logs to Node 1 as shown by the *Binlog dump* process id 357. Node 2 has also processed the binary log of its master Node 1 as shown in the process id 353.

```
mysql> show processlist\G
*************************** 1. row ***************************
     Id: 318
   User: root
   Host: localhost
     db: NULL
Command: Query
   Time: 0
  State: NULL
   Info: show processlist
*************************** 2. row ***************************
     Id: 352
   User: system user
   Host:
     db: NULL
Command: Connect
   Time: 104
  State: Waiting for master to send event
   Info: NULL
*************************** 3. row ***************************
     Id: 353
   User: system user
   Host:
     db: NULL
Command: Connect
   Time: 103
  State: Has read all relay log; waiting for the slave I/O thread to update it
   Info: NULL
*************************** 4. row ***************************
     Id: 357
   User: repl
   Host: ip-72-167-246-49.ip.secureserver.net:34000
     db: NULL
Command: Binlog Dump
   Time: 96
  State: Has sent all binlog to slave; waiting for binlog to be updated
   Info: NULL
4 rows in set (0.00 sec)
```

**Screen-shot 11—18: Show processlist executed on master mobilestatisticsprofessor.us**


## 11.6 Summary

This chapter demonstrated how to establish bi-directional master-master-active-active replication.

# 12 Establishing Master-Master Active-Passive Replication

This chapter presented the steps with example to establish master-master-active-passive replication. Although both servers replicate to each other, the passive server prevents writes by users who do not have special privileges.

## 12.1 Purpose

Purchase of master-master-active-passive replication configuration is to support failover. In case the master fails (to which application was updating), the application can be pointed to the passive master and continue to run.

## 12.2 Approach

- Create replication user account in each master
- Make configuration changes in my.cnf file
  - Assign unique server id
  - To turn binary logging
  - Set *read_only = 1* in the passive server my.cnf setting
  - Optionally assign log file name format and location
  - Optionally assign relay log file name format and location
  - Set read_only in the passive master
  - Set auto_increment_increment and auto_increment_offset
- Restart MySQL server after configuration changes
- Record master log file name and log position.
- Issue change master to command on each master to replicate from the other master.
- Start Slave on each master
- Verify that the passive master is in read_only mode
- Verify whether replication slave is running
- Verify processlist on each master

## 12.3 Logical Architecture

Logical architecture of master-master-active-passive replication configuration is presented below.

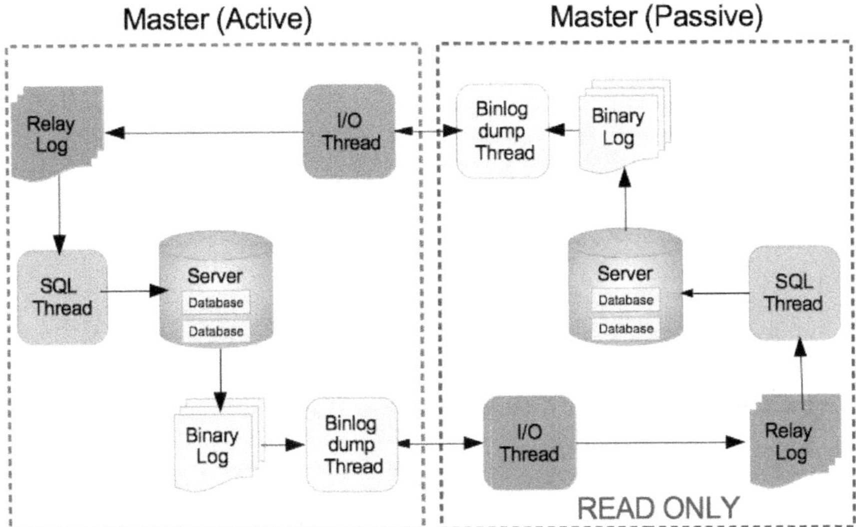


Figure 12—1: Logical Architecture of Master-Master Active-Passive Replication Configuration

## 12.4 Effects of read_only parameter

Read only prevents delete and update type of transactions to be committed into the passive master by non-privileged accounts; such as, replication slave and root.

## 12.5 Physical Architecture

Physical architecture with server details is presented in the diagram below.

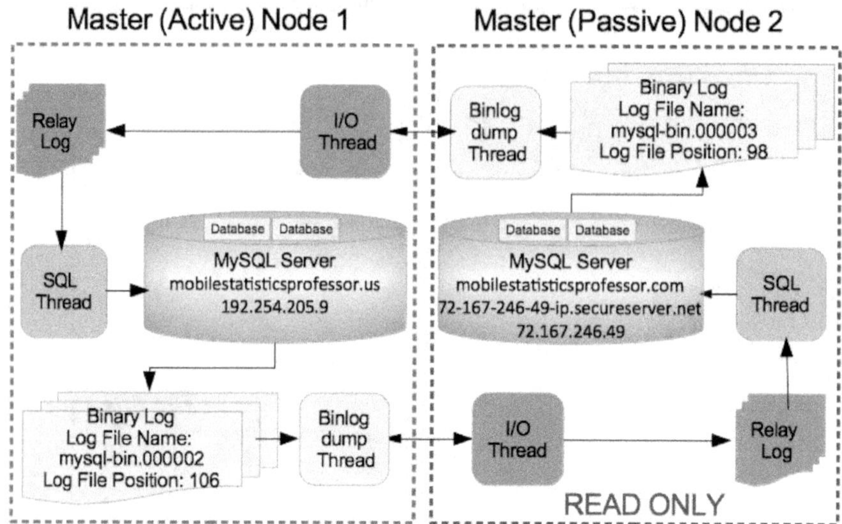


Figure 12—2: Example of Physical Architecture of Master-Master Active-Passive Replication Configuration

MySQL server host details are presented in the table below.

| Srl. No. | Node | Host/IP Address | server_id | Role |
|---|---|---|---|---|
| 1 | Node 1 Active | mobilestatisticsprofessor.us, 192.254.205.9 | 1 | • Node 1 is active master<br>• Node 1 is slave of Node 2 |
| 2 | Node 2 Passive | Mobilestatisticsprofessor.com 72-167-246-49-ip.secureserver.net 72.167.246.49 | 2 | • Node 2 is passive master<br>• Node 2 is slave of Node 1 |

Table 12—1: Master-Master-Active-Passive MySQL Server Configuration

## 12.6 Steps

Create replication user account on both Node 1 and Node 2 unless the replication accounts are already created. Create replication user account on Node 1 allowing Node 2 to read logs from Node 1. Similarly, create replication user account on Node 1 allowing Node 2 to read logs from Node 1. Execute *flush privileges* command if necessary.  Verify the grans to ensure that the replication user has at least *replication slave* grant. The choice of user id and password is up to the DBA to suit the organization's policies and standards.

Create replication user account on Node 1 allowing Node 2 to read logs from Node 1 and flush privileges.

```
mysql> grant replication slave, replication client on *.* to 'repl'@'mobilestati
sticsprofessor.com' identified by 'velcro20';
Query OK, 0 rows affected (0.00 sec)

mysql> flush privileges;
Query OK, 0 rows affected (0.00 sec)
```

**Screen-shot 12—1: Replication user created in master server Node 1 or mobilestatisticsprofessor.us**

Verify that the replication user created in Node 1 has required privileges to facilitate replication.

```
mysql> show grants for 'repl'@'mobilestatisticsprofessor.com'\G
*************************** 1. row ***************************
Grants for repl@mobilestatisticsprofessor.com: GRANT REPLICATION SLAVE, REPLICAT
ION CLIENT ON *.* TO 'repl'@'mobilestatisticsprofessor.com' IDENTIFIED BY PASSWO
RD '5373051f0cfcc009'
1 row in set (0.00 sec)
```

**Screen-shot 12—2: Verifying the replication user account on master mobilestatisticsprofessor.us**

Create replication user account on Node 2 allowing Node 1 to read logs from Node 2 and flush privileges.

```
mysql> grant replication slave, replication client on *.* to 'repl'@'mobilestati
sticsprofessor.us' identified by 'velcro20';
Query OK, 0 rows affected (0.00 sec)

mysql> flush privileges;
Query OK, 0 rows affected (0.00 sec)
```

**Screen-shot 12—3: Added replication user to master mobilestatisticsprofessor.com**

Verify that the replication user created in Node 2 has required privileges to facilitate replication.

```
mysql> show grants for 'repl'@'mobilestatisticsprofessor.us'\G
*************************** 1. row ***************************
Grants for repl@mobilestatisticsprofessor.us: GRANT REPLICATION SLAVE, REPLICATI
ON CLIENT ON *.* TO 'repl'@'mobilestatisticsprofessor.us' IDENTIFIED BY PASSWORD
 '5373051f0cfcc009'
1 row in set (0.00 sec)
```

**Screen-shot 12—4: Verifying the replication user account on master mobilestatisticsprofessor.com**

Make necessary configuration changes to the configuration file my.cnf located on Node 1. At a minimum, the following are added unless already present. Auto_increment_increment and auto_increment_offset is set up to avoid collision of auto_increment key values among the MySQL servers participating in the replication configuration. server_id needs to be unique.  These are the minimum parameters, but these can be expanded to suit the particular need of the organization by the DBA.

*bin_log*
*server_id=1*
*auto_increment_increment=3*
*auto_increment_offset=1*

```
[root@mob ~]# cat /etc/my.cnf
[mysqld]
local-infile=0
max_allowed_packet=16M
set-variable=local-infile=0
datadir=/var/lib/mysql
socket=/var/lib/mysql/mysql.sock
user=mysql
# Default to using old password format for compatibility with mysql 3.x
# clients (those using the mysqlclient10 compatibility package).
old_passwords=1

log_bin=/var/lib/mysql/mysql-bin.log
relay_log=/var/lib/mysql/mysqld-relay-bin.log
server_id=1
expire_logs_days=1
auto_increment_increment=3
auto_increment_offset=1

slave_skip_error=1062

# Disabling symbolic-links is recommended to prevent assorted security risks;
# to do so, uncomment this line:
# symbolic-links=0

#skip-bdb

innodb_buffer_pool_size=2M
innodb_additional_mem_pool_size=500K
innodb_log_buffer_size=500K
innodb_thread_concurrency=2
[mysqld_safe]
log-error=/var/log/mysqld.log
pid-file=/var/run/mysqld/mysqld.pid
#skip-bdb

innodb_buffer_pool_size=2M
innodb_additional_mem_pool_size=500K
innodb_log_buffer_size=500K
innodb_thread_concurrency=2
```

**Screen-shot 12—5: Excerpt of configuration file my.cnf from active master mobilestatisticsprofessor.us**

If my.cnf has been modified on Node 1, restart the MySQL server for the values to take effect.

```
[root@mob ~]# /etc/init.d/mysqld restart
Stopping MySQL:                                            [  OK  ]
Starting MySQL:                                            [  OK  ]
[root@mob ~]#
```

**Screen-shot 12—6: Restarted MySQL Server on master mobilestatisticsprofessor.us**

```
mysql> show variables like 'log_bin';
+---------------+-------+
| Variable_name | Value |
+---------------+-------+
| log_bin       | ON    |
+---------------+-------+
1 row in set (0.00 sec)

mysql> show variables like 'server_id';
+---------------+-------+
| Variable_name | Value |
+---------------+-------+
| server_id     | 1     |
+---------------+-------+
1 row in set (0.00 sec)

mysql> show variables like 'auto_increment_increment';
+--------------------------+-------+
| Variable_name            | Value |
+--------------------------+-------+
| auto_increment_increment | 3     |
+--------------------------+-------+
1 row in set (0.00 sec)

mysql> show variables like 'auto_increment_offset';
+-----------------------+-------+
| Variable_name         | Value |
+-----------------------+-------+
| auto_increment_offset | 1     |
+-----------------------+-------+
1 row in set (0.00 sec)
```

**Screen-shot 12—7: Checking session variables log_bin, server_id. auto_increment_increment and auto_increment_offset on master mobilestatisticsprofessor.us**

Verify log_bin, auto_increment_increment and auto_increment_offset parameters after the server is restarted to ensure that the parameters have been set correctly in Node 1.

Make necessary configuration changes to the configuration file my.cnf located on Node 1. At a minimum, the following are added unless already present. Auto_increment_increment and auto_increment_offset is set up to avoid collision of auto_increment key values among the MySQL servers participating in the replication configuration. server_id needs to be unique.  These are the minimum parameters, but these can be expanded to suit the particular need of the organization by the DBA.

*bin_log*
*server_id=2*
*auto_increment_increment=3*
*auto_increment_offset=2*
*__read_only=1__*

```
[mysqld]
datadir=/var/lib/mysql
socket=/var/lib/mysql/mysql.sock
user=mysql
# Default to using old password format for compatibility with mysql 3.x
# clients (those using the mysqlclient10 compatibility package).
old_passwords=1

log_bin=/var/lib/mysql/mysql-bin.log
server_id=2
expire_logs_days=1
read_only=1

[mysqld_safe]
log-error=/var/log/mysqld.log
pid-file=/var/run/mysqld/mysqld.pid
```

**Screen-shot 12—8: Excerpt of configuration file my.cnf from passive master mobilestatisticsprofessor.com displaying read_only parameter**

If my.cnf has been modified on Node 2, restart the MySQL server for the values to take effect.

*$/etc/init.d/mysqld restart*

```
[root@ip-72-167-246-49 ~]# /etc/init.d/mysqld restart
Stopping MySQL:                                          [  OK  ]
Starting MySQL:                                          [  OK  ]
```

**Screen-shot 12—9: Restarting MySQL Server on the passive master mobilestatisticsprofessor.com**

Verify that the Node 2 server is operating on a **read_only** mode. Additionally, verify log_bin, auto_increment_increment and auto_increment_offset parameters after the server is restarted to ensure that the parameters have been set correctly in Node 2.

```
[root@ip-72-167-246-49 ~]# mysql -uroot -p
Enter password:
Welcome to the MySQL monitor.  Commands end with ; or \g.
Your MySQL connection id is 4
Server version: 5.0.77-log Source distribution

Type 'help;' or '\h' for help. Type '\c' to clear the buffer.

mysql> show variables like 'read_only';
+---------------+-------+
| Variable_name | Value |
+---------------+-------+
| read_only     | ON    |
+---------------+-------+
1 row in set (0.00 sec)
```

**Screen-shot 12—10: Verifying read_only status of passive master mobilestatisticsprofessor.com**

Record log file name and position on Node 1 by executing *show master status* command.

```
mysql> show master status;
+------------------+----------+--------------+------------------+
| File             | Position | Binlog_Do_DB | Binlog_Ignore_DB |
+------------------+----------+--------------+------------------+
| mysql-bin.000002 |      106 |              |                  |
+------------------+----------+--------------+------------------+
1 row in set (0.00 sec)
```

**Screen-shot 12—11: Show master status on passive master mobilestatisticsprofessor.com**

Similarly, record log file name and position on Node 2 by executing *show master status* command.

```
mysql> show master status;
+------------------+----------+--------------+------------------+
| File             | Position | Binlog_Do_DB | Binlog_Ignore_DB |
+------------------+----------+--------------+------------------+
| mysql-bin.000003 |       98 |              |                  |
+------------------+----------+--------------+------------------+
1 row in set (0.00 sec)
```

**Screen-shot 12—12: Show master status executed on passive master mobilestatisticsprofessor.com**

Verify slave status on Node 1. Slave I/O and SQL should not be running at this stage.

```
mysql> show slave status\G
*************************** 1. row ***************************
               Slave_IO_State:
                  Master_Host: mobilestatisticsprofessor.com
                  Master_User: repl
                  Master_Port: 3306
                Connect_Retry: 60
              Master_Log_File: mysql-bin.000002
          Read_Master_Log_Pos: 98
               Relay_Log_File: mysqld-relay-bin.000002
                Relay_Log_Pos: 243
        Relay_Master_Log_File: mysql-bin.000002
             Slave_IO_Running: No
            Slave_SQL_Running: No
              Replicate_Do_DB:
          Replicate_Ignore_DB:
           Replicate_Do_Table:
       Replicate_Ignore_Table:
      Replicate_Wild_Do_Table:
  Replicate_Wild_Ignore_Table:
                   Last_Errno: 0
                   Last_Error:
                 Skip_Counter: 0
          Exec_Master_Log_Pos: 98
              Relay_Log_Space: 399
              Until_Condition: None
               Until_Log_File:
                Until_Log_Pos: 0
           Master_SSL_Allowed: No
           Master_SSL_CA_File:
           Master_SSL_CA_Path:
              Master_SSL_Cert:
            Master_SSL_Cipher:
               Master_SSL_Key:
        Seconds_Behind_Master: NULL
Master_SSL_Verify_Server_Cert: No
                Last_IO_Errno: 0
                Last_IO_Error:
               Last_SQL_Errno: 0
               Last_SQL_Error:
1 row in set (0.00 sec)
```

**Screen-shot 12—13: Show master status executed on active master mobilestatisticsprofessor.us**

Execute *change master* command on Node 1 to establish replication from Node 2. Then, execute *start slave* on Node 1 to start replicating.

```
mysql> change master to master_host='mobilestatisticsprofessor.com', master_user='repl', master_password='velcr
o20', master_log_file='mysql-bin.000003', master_log_pos=98;
Query OK, 0 rows affected (0.01 sec)

mysql> start slave;
Query OK, 0 rows affected (0.00 sec)
```

**Screen-shot 12—14: Change master command executed on active master mobilestatisticsprofessor.us and slave is started**

Verify slave status on Node 1. Slave I/O and SQL threads need to run without error for the slave to replicate from master successfully. Optionally, *execute show processlist* to check the processes running on the server. Screen-shot displaying output of show processlist is not presented here.

```
mysql> show slave status\G
*************************** 1. row ***************************
               Slave_IO_State: Waiting for master to send event
                  Master_Host: mobilestatisticsprofessor.com
                  Master_User: repl
                  Master_Port: 3306
                Connect_Retry: 60
              Master_Log_File: mysql-bin.000003
          Read_Master_Log_Pos: 98
               Relay_Log_File: mysqld-relay-bin.000002
                Relay_Log_Pos: 243
        Relay_Master_Log_File: mysql-bin.000003
             Slave_IO_Running: Yes
            Slave_SQL_Running: Yes
              Replicate_Do_DB:
          Replicate_Ignore_DB:
           Replicate_Do_Table:
       Replicate_Ignore_Table:
      Replicate_Wild_Do_Table:
  Replicate_Wild_Ignore_Table:
                   Last_Errno: 0
                   Last_Error:
                 Skip_Counter: 0
          Exec_Master_Log_Pos: 98
              Relay_Log_Space: 399
              Until_Condition: None
               Until_Log_File:
                Until_Log_Pos: 0
           Master_SSL_Allowed: No
           Master_SSL_CA_File:
           Master_SSL_CA_Path:
              Master_SSL_Cert:
            Master_SSL_Cipher:
               Master_SSL_Key:
        Seconds_Behind_Master: 0
Master_SSL_Verify_Server_Cert: No
                Last_IO_Errno: 0
                Last_IO_Error:
               Last_SQL_Errno: 0
               Last_SQL_Error:
1 row in set (0.00 sec)
```

**Screen-shot 12—15: Show slave status command executed on active master mobilestatisticsprofessor.us**

Execute *change master* command on Node 2 to establish replication from Node 1. Then, execute *start slave* on Node 2 to start replicating.

```
mysql>  change master to master_host='mobilestatisticsprofessor.us', master_user='repl', mas
ter_password='velcro20', master_log_file='mysql-bin.000002', master_log_pos=106;
Query OK, 0 rows affected (0.21 sec)

mysql> start slave;
Query OK, 0 rows affected (0.00 sec)
```

**Screen-shot 12—16: Change master command issued on passive master mobilestatisticsprofessor.com and slave started**

Verify slave status on Node 2. Slave I/O and SQL threads need to run without error for the slave to replicate from master successfully. Optionally, *execute show processlist* to check the processes running on the server. Screen-shot displaying output of show processlist is not presented here.

```
mysql> show slave status\G
*************************** 1. row ***************************
               Slave_IO_State: Waiting for master to send event
                  Master_Host: mobilestatisticsprofessor.us
                  Master_User: repl
                  Master_Port: 3306
                Connect_Retry: 60
              Master_Log_File: mysql-bin.000002
          Read_Master_Log_Pos: 106
               Relay_Log_File: mysqld-relay-bin.000002
                Relay_Log_Pos: 243
        Relay_Master_Log_File: mysql-bin.000002
             Slave_IO_Running: Yes
            Slave_SQL_Running: Yes
              Replicate_Do_DB:
          Replicate_Ignore_DB:
           Replicate_Do_Table:
       Replicate_Ignore_Table:
      Replicate_Wild_Do_Table:
  Replicate_Wild_Ignore_Table:
                   Last_Errno: 0
                   Last_Error:
                 Skip_Counter: 0
          Exec_Master_Log_Pos: 106
              Relay_Log_Space: 243
              Until_Condition: None
               Until_Log_File:
                Until_Log_Pos: 0
           Master_SSL_Allowed: No
           Master_SSL_CA_File:
           Master_SSL_CA_Path:
              Master_SSL_Cert:
            Master_SSL_Cipher:
               Master_SSL_Key:
        Seconds_Behind_Master: 0
1 row in set (0.00 sec)
```

**Screen-shot 12—17: Show processlist command executed on passive master mobilestatisticsprofessor.com**

## 12.7 Summary

This chapter demonstrated how to establish master-master-active-passive replication.

# 13 Establishing Master-Slave Replication

This chapter presents the classic replication configuration master-slave where one server (master) replicates its binary log events to another (slave).

## 13.1 Purpose

The purpose of master-slave replication is to create an effective backup or to create a database for reporting or analysis.

## 13.2 Approach

Approach to establishing master-slave replication is presented below.

- Create replication user account in the master
- Make configuration changes in master my.cnf file
  - Master
    - Assign unique server id
    - To turn binary logging on
    - Optionally assign log file name format and location
  - Slave
    - Assign unique server id
    - Optionally assign relay log file name format and location
    - Optionally turn read_only on

- Restart MySQL servers after configuration changes
- Record master log file name and log position.
- Issue change master to command on the slave to replicate from master
- *Start Slave* on slave
- Verify whether replication slave is running on the slave
- Verify processlist on each server

## 13.3 Logical Architecture

Logical architecture of master-slave replication configuration is presented below.

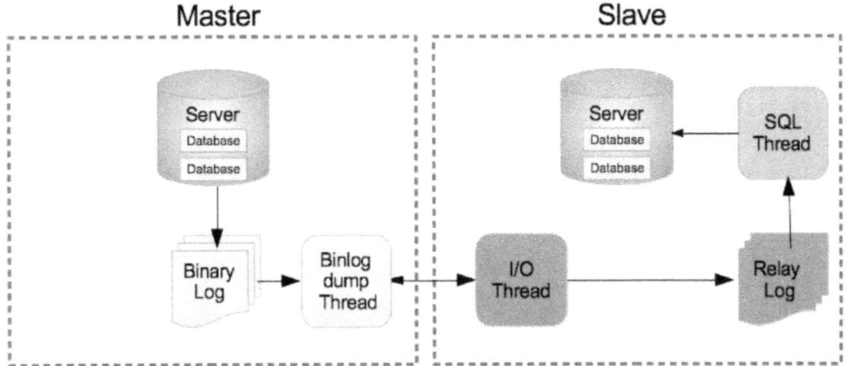


Figure 13—1: Logical Architecture of Master-Slave Replication Configuration

## 13.4 Physical Architecture

Physical architecture diagram o master-slave replication configuration is presented below.

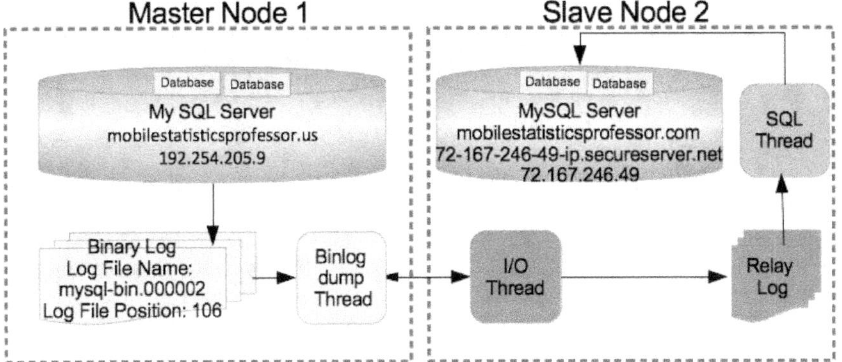


Figure 13—2: Example of Physical Architecture of Master-Slave Replication Configuration

MySQL server host details are presented in the table below.

| Srl. No. | Node | Host/IP Address | server_id | Role |
|---|---|---|---|---|
| 1 | Node 1 Active | mobilestatisticsprofessor.us, 192.254.205.9 | 1 | • Node 1 is master of Node 2 |
| 2 | Node 2 Passive | Mobilestatisticsprofessor.com 72-167-246-49-ip.secureserver.net 72.167.246.49 | 2 | • Node 2 is slave of Node 1 |

Table 13—1: Master-Master-Active-Passive MySQL Server Configuration

## 13.5 Steps

Create replication user account on Node 1 unless the replication accounts are already created. Create replication user account on Node 1 allowing Node 2 to read logs from Node 1. Execute *flush privileges* command if necessary.  Verify the grans to ensure that the replication user has at least *replication slave* grant. The choice of user id and password is up to the DBA to suit the organization's policies and standards.

Create replication user account on Node 1 allowing Node 2 to read logs from Node 1 and flush privileges.

```
mysql> grant replication slave, replication client on *.* to 'repl'@'mobilestati
sticsprofessor.com' identified by 'velcro20';
Query OK, 0 rows affected (0.00 sec)

mysql> flush privileges;
Query OK, 0 rows affected (0.00 sec)
```

**Screen-shot 13—1: Replication user created in master server Node 1 or mobilestatisticsprofessor.us**

Verify that the replication user created in Node 1 has required privileges to facilitate replication.

```
mysql> show grants for 'repl'@'mobilestatisticsprofessor.com'\G
*************************** 1. row ***************************
Grants for repl@mobilestatisticsprofessor.com: GRANT REPLICATION SLAVE, REPLICAT
ION CLIENT ON *.* TO 'repl'@'mobilestatisticsprofessor.com' IDENTIFIED BY PASSWO
RD '5373051f0cfcc009'
1 row in set (0.00 sec)
```

**Screen-shot 13—2: Verifying the replication user account on master mobilestatisticsprofessor.us**

Make necessary configuration changes to the configuration file my.cnf located on Node 1. At a minimum, the following are added unless already present. Auto_increment_increment and auto_increment_offset can be set up to avoid collision of auto_increment key values among the MySQL servers participating in the replication configuration. server_id needs to be unique.  These are the minimum parameters, but these can be expanded to suit the particular need of the organization by the DBA.

*bin_log*
*server_id=1*

```
[mysqld]
local-infile=0
max_allowed_packet=16M
set-variable=local-infile=0
datadir=/var/lib/mysql
socket=/var/lib/mysql/mysql.sock
user=mysql
# Default to using old password format for compatibility with mysql 3.x
# clients (those using the mysqlclient10 compatibility package).
old_passwords=1

log_bin=/var/lib/mysql/mysql-bin.log
server_id=1
expire_logs_days=1
```

**Screen-shot 13—3: Excerpt of configuration file my.cnf of the master mobilestatisticsprofessor.us**

If my.cnf has been modified on Node 1, restart the MySQL server for the values to take effect.

```
[root@mob ~]# /etc/init.d/mysqld restart
Stopping MySQL:                                            [  OK  ]
Starting MySQL:                                            [  OK  ]
[root@mob ~]#
```

**Screen-shot 13—4: Restarted MySQL Server on master mobilestatisticsprofessor.us**

Verify log_bin, auto_increment_increment and auto_increment_offset parameters after the server is restarted to ensure that the parameters have been set correctly in Node 1.

```
mysql> show variables like 'log_bin';
+---------------+-------+
| Variable_name | Value |
+---------------+-------+
| log_bin       | ON    |
+---------------+-------+
1 row in set (0.00 sec)

mysql> show variables like 'server_id';
+---------------+-------+
| Variable_name | Value |
+---------------+-------+
| server_id     | 1     |
+---------------+-------+
1 row in set (0.00 sec)

mysql> show variables like 'auto_increment_increment';
+--------------------------+-------+
| Variable_name            | Value |
+--------------------------+-------+
| auto_increment_increment | 3     |
+--------------------------+-------+
1 row in set (0.00 sec)

mysql> show variables like 'auto_increment_offset';
+-----------------------+-------+
| Variable_name         | Value |
+-----------------------+-------+
| auto_increment_offset | 1     |
+-----------------------+-------+
1 row in set (0.00 sec)
```

**Screen-shot 13—5: Checking session variables log_bin, server_id. auto_increment_increment and auto_increment_offset on master mobilestatisticsprofessor.us**

Make necessary configuration changes to the configuration file my.cnf located on Node 2. At a minimum, the following are added unless already present. Auto_increment_increment and auto_increment_offset can be set up to avoid collision of auto_increment key values among the MySQL servers participating in the replication configuration. server_id needs to be unique.  Read_only parameter can be set to 1 to place the slave in "read only" mode. These are the minimum parameters, but these can be expanded to suit the particular need of the organization by the DBA.

*server_id=2*
*read_only=1*

```
[mysqld]
datadir=/var/lib/mysql
socket=/var/lib/mysql/mysql.sock
user=mysql
# Default to using old password format for compatibility with mysql 3.x
# clients (those using the mysqlclient10 compatibility package).
old_passwords=1

#log_bin=/var/lib/mysql/mysql-bin.log
#relay_log=/var/lib/mysql/mysqld-relay-bin.log
#log_slave_updates
server_id=2
#expire_logs_days=1
read_only=1
#auto_increment_increment=3
#auto_increment_offset=2
```

**Screen-shot 13—6: Excerpt of configuration file my.cnf from the slave mobilestatisticsprofessor.com**

If my.cnf has been modified on Node 2, restart the MySQL server for the values to take effect.

*$/etc/init.d/mysqld restart*

```
[root@ip-72-167-246-49 ~]# /etc/init.d/mysqld restart
Stopping MySQL:                                        [  OK  ]
Starting MySQL:                                        [  OK  ]
```

**Screen-shot 13—7: Restarting MySQL Server on the passive master mobilestatisticsprofessor.com**

Verify that the Node 2 server is operating on a **read_only** mode. Additionally, verify auto_increment_increment and auto_increment_offset parameters after the server is restarted to ensure that the parameters have been set correctly in Node 2.

```
[root@ip-72-167-246-49 ~]# mysql -uroot -p
Enter password:
Welcome to the MySQL monitor.  Commands end with ; or \g.
Your MySQL connection id is 4
Server version: 5.0.77-log Source distribution

Type 'help;' or '\h' for help. Type '\c' to clear the buffer.

mysql> show variables like 'read_only';
+---------------+-------+
| Variable_name | Value |
+---------------+-------+
| read_only     | ON    |
+---------------+-------+
1 row in set (0.00 sec)
```

**Screen-shot 13—8: Verifying read_only status of passive master mobilestatisticsprofessor.com**

Record log file name and position on Node 1 by executing *show master status* command.

```
mysql> show master status;
+------------------+----------+--------------+------------------+
| File             | Position | Binlog_Do_DB | Binlog_Ignore_DB |
+------------------+----------+--------------+------------------+
| mysql-bin.000002 |      106 |              |                  |
+------------------+----------+--------------+------------------+
1 row in set (0.00 sec)
```

**Screen-shot 13—9: Show master status executed on master mobilestatisticsprofessor.us**

Verify slave status on Node 2.  Slave I/O and SQL threads must not be running. Optionally, *execute show processlist* to check the processes running on the server. Screen-shot displaying output of show processlist is not presented here.

```
mysql> show slave status\G
*************************** 1. row ***************************
               Slave_IO_State:
                  Master_Host: mobilestatisticsprofessor.us
                  Master_User: repl
                  Master_Port: 3306
                Connect_Retry: 60
              Master_Log_File: mysql-bin.000002
          Read_Master_Log_Pos: 106
               Relay_Log_File: mysqld-relay-bin.000004
                Relay_Log_Pos: 243
        Relay_Master_Log_File: mysql-bin.000002
             Slave_IO_Running: No
            Slave_SQL_Running: No
              Replicate_Do_DB:
          Replicate_Ignore_DB:
           Replicate_Do_Table:
       Replicate_Ignore_Table:
      Replicate_Wild_Do_Table:
  Replicate_Wild_Ignore_Table:
                   Last_Errno: 0
                   Last_Error:
                 Skip_Counter: 0
          Exec_Master_Log_Pos: 106
              Relay_Log_Space: 243
              Until_Condition: None
               Until_Log_File:
                Until_Log_Pos: 0
           Master_SSL_Allowed: No
           Master_SSL_CA_File:
           Master_SSL_CA_Path:
              Master_SSL_Cert:
            Master_SSL_Cipher:
               Master_SSL_Key:
        Seconds_Behind_Master: NULL
1 row in set (0.00 sec)
```

**Screen-shot 13—10: Show slave status command executed on slave mobilestatisticsprofessor.com**

Execute *change master* command on Node 2 to establish replication from Node 1. Then, execute *start slave* on Node 2 to start replicating.

```
mysql> change master to master_host='mobilestatisticsprofessor.us', master_user='repl', master_password='velcro20'
, master_log_file='mysql-bin.000002', master_log_pos=106;
Query OK, 0 rows affected (0.17 sec)

mysql> start slave;
Query OK, 0 rows affected (0.00 sec)
```

**Screen-shot 13—11: Change master command executed on slave mobilestatisticsprofessor.com**

Verify slave status on Node 2. Slave I/O and SQL threads need to run without error for the slave to replicate from master successfully.

```
mysql> show slave status\G
*************************** 1. row ***************************
               Slave_IO_State: Waiting for master to send event
                  Master_Host: mobilestatisticsprofessor.us
                  Master_User: repl
                  Master_Port: 3306
                Connect_Retry: 60
              Master_Log_File: mysql-bin.000002
          Read_Master_Log_Pos: 106
               Relay_Log_File: mysqld-relay-bin.000002
                Relay_Log_Pos: 243
        Relay_Master_Log_File: mysql-bin.000002
             Slave_IO_Running: Yes
            Slave_SQL_Running: Yes
              Replicate_Do_DB:
          Replicate_Ignore_DB:
           Replicate_Do_Table:
       Replicate_Ignore_Table:
      Replicate_Wild_Do_Table:
  Replicate_Wild_Ignore_Table:
                   Last_Errno: 0
                   Last_Error:
                 Skip_Counter: 0
          Exec_Master_Log_Pos: 106
              Relay_Log_Space: 243
              Until_Condition: None
               Until_Log_File:
                Until_Log_Pos: 0
           Master_SSL_Allowed: No
           Master_SSL_CA_File:
           Master_SSL_CA_Path:
              Master_SSL_Cert:
            Master_SSL_Cipher:
               Master_SSL_Key:
        Seconds_Behind_Master: 0
1 row in set (0.00 sec)
```

**Screen-shot 13—12: Show slave status executed on slave mobilestatisticsprofessor.com**

Optionally, *execute show processlist* on Node 2 to check the processes running on the server. Screen-shot displaying output of show processlist is not presented here.

```
mysql> show processlist\G
*************************** 1. row ***************************
     Id: 4
   User: root
   Host: localhost
     db: NULL
Command: Query
   Time: 0
  State: NULL
   Info: show processlist
*************************** 2. row ***************************
     Id: 6
   User: system user
   Host:
     db: NULL
Command: Connect
   Time: 72
  State: Waiting for master to send event
   Info: NULL
*************************** 3. row ***************************
     Id: 7
   User: system user
   Host:
     db: NULL
Command: Connect
   Time: 71
  State: Has read all relay log; waiting for the slave I/O thread to update it
   Info: NULL
3 rows in set (0.00 sec)
```

**Screen-shot 13—13: Show processlist command executed on slave mobilestatisticsprofessor.com**

## 13.6 Summary

This chapter demonstrated how to establish replication between a master and a slave.

# 14 Establishing Master-Slave-Slave Chain Replication

This chapter describes how to establish master-slave-slave replication where the slave replicates to other slaves in a chain of slaves.

## 14.1 Purpose

Master-slave-slave type of configuration can be used for distributing backups across multiple servers.

## 14.2 Approach

The approach to establish master-slave-slave configuration is as follows.

- Create replication user account
    - In the master for the slave to replicate from master
    - In the slave (replicating from the master) to allow the other slave to replicate from the slave
- Make configuration changes in master my.cnf file
    - Master
        - Assign unique server id
        - Turn binary logging on
        - Optionally assign binary log file name format and location
        - Optionally assign relay log file name format and location
    - Slave (replicating from master)
        - Assign unique server id
        - To turn binary logging on
        - Turn log_slave_update on
        - Optionally assign binary log file name format and location
        - Optionally assign relay log file name format and location
        - Optionally turn read_only on
    - Slave (replicating from slave)
        - Assign unique server id
        - Optionally assign relay log file name format and location
        - Optionally turn read_only on
- Restart MySQL servers after configuration changes
- Record log file name and log position of
    - master and
    - slave (replicating from master).
- Execute change master to command on
    - slave (replicating from master) to read log from the master.
    - slave (replicating from slave) to read log from slave (replicating from master)
- *Start slave* on both slaves

- Verify whether replication slave is running on both slaves
- Verify processlist on each server

## 14.3  Logical Architecture

Logical architecture diagram of master-slave-slave configuration is presented below.

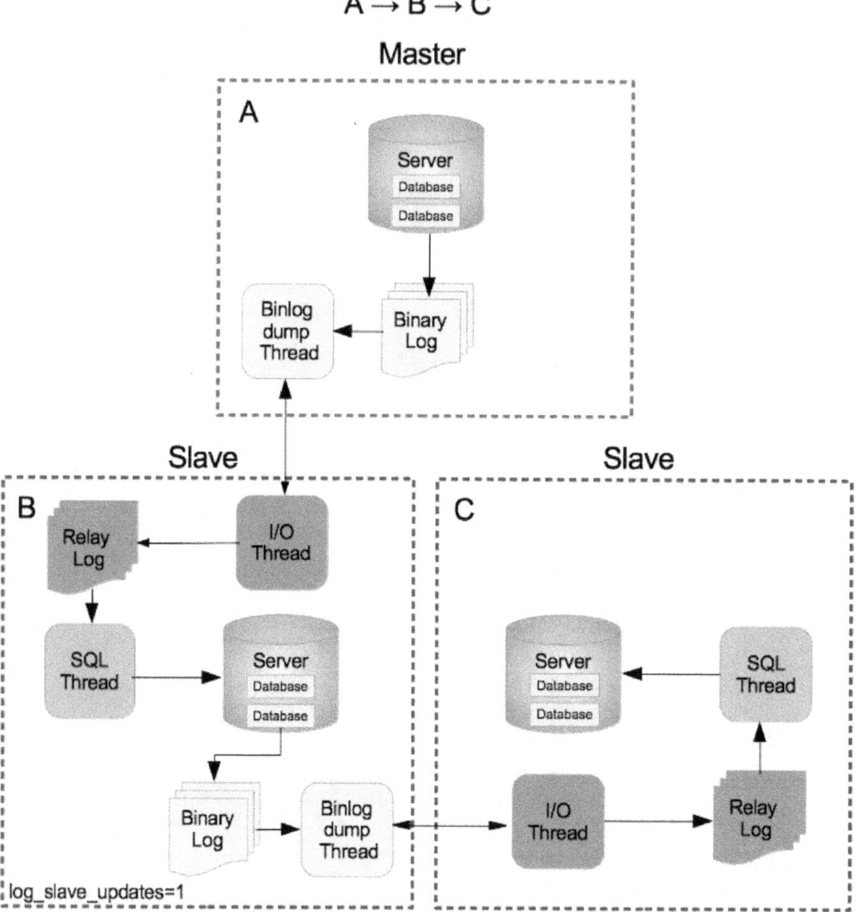


Figure 14—1: Logical Architecture of Master Replicating to a Slave and the Slave is replicating to another slave in a chain

## 14.4  Physical Architecture

Physical diagram of master and 2 slaves participating in master-slave-slave replication is presented below.

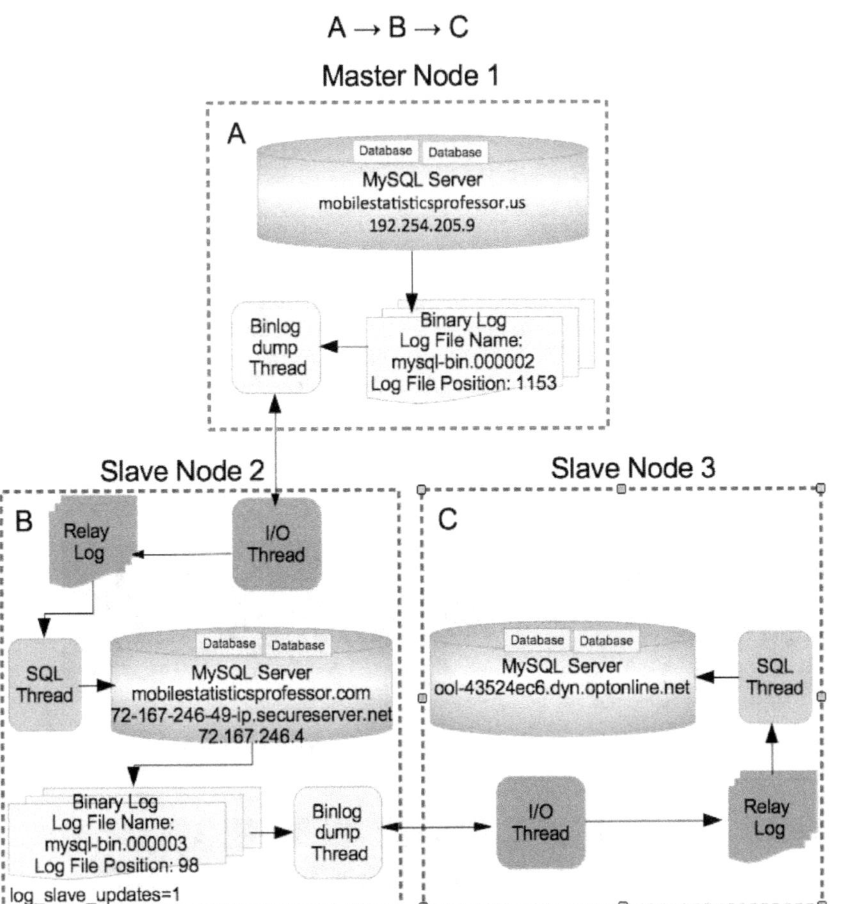


**Figure 14—2: Example of Physical Architecture of a Master replicating to a Slave and the Slave is replicating to another Slave in a chain**

MySQL server host details are presented in the table below.

| Srl. No. | Node | Host/IP Address | server_id | Role |
|---|---|---|---|---|
| 1 | Node 1 | mobilestatisticsprofessor.us, 192.254.205.9 | 1 | • Node 1 is master of Node 2 |
| 2 | Node 2 | Mobilestatisticsprofessor.com 72-167-246-49-ip.secureserver.net 72.167.246.49 | 2 | • Node 2 is slave of Node 1<br>• Node 2 is master of |

| Srl. No. | Node | Host/IP Address | server_id | Role |
|---|---|---|---|---|
| | | | | Node 3 |
| 3 | Node 2 | ool-43524ec6.dyn.optonline.net | 3 | • Node 2 is slave of Node 1<br>• Node 2 is master of Node 3 |

Table 14—1: Master-Slave-Slave MySQL Server Configuration

Create replication user account on Node 1 unless the replication accounts are already created. Create replication user account on Node 1 allowing Node 2 to read logs from Node 1. Execute *flush privileges* command if necessary. Verify the grans to ensure that the replication user has at least *replication slave* grant. The choice of user id and password is up to the DBA to suit the organization's policies and standards.

Create replication user account on Node 1 allowing Node 2 to read logs from Node 1 and flush privileges.

```
mysql> grant replication slave, replication client on *.* to 'repl'@'mobilestati
sticsprofessor.com' identified by 'velcro20';
Query OK, 0 rows affected (0.00 sec)

mysql> flush privileges;
Query OK, 0 rows affected (0.00 sec)
```

Screen-shot 14—1: Adding replication user on master mobilestatisticsprofessor.us

Verify that the replication user created in Node 1 has required privileges to facilitate replication.

```
mysql> show grants for 'repl'@'mobilestatisticsprofessor.com'\G
*************************** 1. row ***************************
Grants for repl@mobilestatisticsprofessor.com: GRANT REPLICATION SLAVE, REPLICAT
ION CLIENT ON *.* TO 'repl'@'mobilestatisticsprofessor.com' IDENTIFIED BY PASSWO
RD '5373051f0cfcc009'
1 row in set (0.00 sec)
```

Screen-shot 14—2: Verifying grants of replication user created on master mobilestatisticsprofessor.us

Create replication user account on Node 2 allowing Node 3 to read logs from Node 2 and flush privileges.

```
mysql> grant replication client, replication slave on *.* to 'repl'@'ool-43524ec6.dyn.optonline.net' id
entified by 'velcro20';
Query OK, 0 rows affected (0.00 sec)

mysql> flush privileges;
Query OK, 0 rows affected (0.00 sec)
```

Screen-shot 14—3: Creating replication user on slave mobilestatisticsprofessor.com to replicate to slave ool-43524ec6.dyn.optonline.net

Verify that the replication user created in Node 2 has required privileges to facilitate replication.

```
mysql> show grants for 'repl'@'ool-43524ec6.dyn.optonline.net'\G
*************************** 1. row ***************************
Grants for repl@ool-43524ec6.dyn.optonline.net: GRANT REPLICATION SLAVE, REPLICA
TION CLIENT ON *.* TO 'repl'@'ool-43524ec6.dyn.optonline.net' IDENTIFIED BY PASS
WORD '5373051f0cfcc009'
1 row in set (0.00 sec)
```
**Screen-shot 14—4: Verifying replication user grants on mobilestatisticsprofessor.com**

Make necessary configuration changes to the configuration file my.cnf located on Node 1. At a minimum, the following are added unless already present. Auto_increment_increment and auto_increment_offset can be set up to avoid collision of auto_increment key values among the MySQL servers participating in the replication configuration. server_id needs to be unique.  These are the minimum parameters, but these can be expanded to suit the particular need of the organization by the DBA.

*bin_log*
*server_id=1*

```
[mysqld]
local-infile=0
max_allowed_packet=16M
set-variable=local-infile=0
datadir=/var/lib/mysql
socket=/var/lib/mysql/mysql.sock
user=mysql
# Default to using old password format for compatibility with mysql 3.x
# clients (those using the mysqlclient10 compatibility package).
old_passwords=1

log_bin=/var/lib/mysql/mysql-bin.log
server_id=1
expire_logs_days=1
```
**Screen-shot 14—5: Excerpt of configuration file my.cnf from the master mobilestatisticsprofessor.us**

If my.cnf has been modified on Node 1, restart the MySQL server for the values to take effect.

```
[root@mob ~]# /etc/init.d/mysqld restart
Stopping MySQL:                                            [  OK  ]
Starting MySQL:                                            [  OK  ]
[root@mob ~]#
```
**Screen-shot 14—6: Restarted MySQL Server on master mobilestatisticsprofessor.us**

Make necessary configuration changes to the configuration file my.cnf located on Node 2. At a minimum, the following are added unless already present. Auto_increment_increment and auto_increment_offset can be set up to avoid collision of auto_increment key values among the MySQL servers participating in the replication configuration. server_id needs to be unique.  Log_slave_update is added to enable Node 2 to replicate its log to Node 3. *log_bin* must be turned on in conjunction with *log_slave_udpates* to facilitate replication. Optionally, the server can be placed in "read only" mode. These are the minimum parameters, but these can be expanded to suit the particular need of the organization by the DBA.

*bin_log*
*server_id=2*
*log_slave_updates*

```
[altman@ip-72-167-246-49 ~]$ su -
Password:
[root@ip-72-167-246-49 ~]# vi /etc/my.cnf
[root@ip-72-167-246-49 ~]# cat /etc/my.cnf
[mysqld]
datadir=/var/lib/mysql
socket=/var/lib/mysql/mysql.sock
user=mysql
# Default to using old password format for compatibility with mysql 3.x
# clients (those using the mysqlclient10 compatibility package).
old_passwords=1

log_bin=/var/lib/mysql/mysql-bin.log
log_slave_updates
server_id=2
expire_logs_days=1
#read_only=1

[mysqld_safe]
log-error=/var/log/mysqld.log
pid-file=/var/run/mysqld/mysqld.pid
[root@ip-72-167-246-49 ~]# /etc/init.d/mysqld restart
Stopping MySQL:                                          [  OK  ]
```

**Screen-shot 14—7: Adding slave_update to configuration file my.cnf of replicating slave mobilestatisticsprofessor.com to replicate to its slave ool-43524ec6.dyn.optonline.net**

On Node 2, verify that log_bin and log_slave_update parameters are turned on

```
mysql> show variables like 'log_bin';
+---------------+-------+
| Variable_name | Value |
+---------------+-------+
| log_bin       | ON    |
+---------------+-------+
1 row in set (0.00 sec)

mysql> show variables like 'log_slave_updates';
+-------------------+-------+
| Variable_name     | Value |
+-------------------+-------+
| log_slave_updates | ON    |
+-------------------+-------+
1 row in set (0.00 sec)
```

**Screen-shot 14—8: Verifying status of binary logging and slave updates on replicating slave mobilestatisticsprofessor.com**

Make necessary configuration changes to the configuration file my.cnf located on Node 3. At a minimum, the following are added unless already present. Auto_increment_increment and auto_increment_offset can be set up to avoid collision of auto_increment key values among the MySQL servers participating in the replication configuration. server_id needs to be unique. Optionally, the server can be placed in "read only" mode. These are the minimum parameters, but these can be expanded to suit the particular need of the organization by the DBA. Screenshot of my.cnf change is not displayed here.

*server_id=3*

If my.cnf has been modified on Node 3, restart the MySQL server for the values to take effect. The output of execution of restarting MySQL server is not displayed here.

*$/etc/init.d/mysqld restart*

Record log file name and position on Node 1 by executing *show master status* command.

```
mysql> show master status;
+------------------+----------+--------------+------------------+
| File             | Position | Binlog_Do_DB | Binlog_Ignore_DB |
+------------------+----------+--------------+------------------+
| mysql-bin.000002 |      770 |              |                  |
+------------------+----------+--------------+------------------+
1 row in set (0.00 sec)
```

**Screen-shot 14—9: Show master status executed on master mobilestatisticsprofessor.us**

Record log file name and position on Node 2 by executing *show master status* command.

```
mysql> show master status;
+------------------+----------+--------------+------------------+
| File             | Position | Binlog_Do_DB | Binlog_Ignore_DB |
+------------------+----------+--------------+------------------+
| mysql-bin.000001 |       98 |              |                  |
+------------------+----------+--------------+------------------+
1 row in set (0.00 sec)
```

**Screen-shot 14—10: Show master status executed on replicating slave mobilestatisticsprofessor.com**

Execute *change master* command on Node 2 to establish replication from Node 1. Then, execute *start slave* on Node 2 to start replicating.

```
mysql> change master to master_host='mobilestatisticsprofessor.us', master_user='repl', master_password='velcro20', master_log_file='mysql-bin.000002', master_log_pos=770;
Query OK, 0 rows affected (7.82 sec)

mysql> start slave;
Query OK, 0 rows affected (0.00 sec)
```

**Screen-shot 14—11: Change master command executed on replicating slave mobilestatisticsprofessor.com**

Verify slave status on Node 2.  Slave I/O and SQL threads need to run without error for the slave to replicate from master successfully.  Additionally, *show processlist* command can be executed to verify processes running.

```
mysql> show slave status\G
*************************** 1. row ***************************
               Slave_IO_State: Waiting for master to send event
                  Master_Host: mobilestatisticsprofessor.us
                  Master_User: repl
                  Master_Port: 3306
                Connect_Retry: 60
              Master_Log_File: mysql-bin.000002
          Read_Master_Log_Pos: 770
               Relay_Log_File: mysqld-relay-bin.000002
                Relay_Log_Pos: 243
        Relay_Master_Log_File: mysql-bin.000002
             Slave_IO_Running: Yes
            Slave_SQL_Running: Yes
              Replicate_Do_DB:
          Replicate_Ignore_DB:
           Replicate_Do_Table:
       Replicate_Ignore_Table:
      Replicate_Wild_Do_Table:
  Replicate_Wild_Ignore_Table:
                   Last_Errno: 0
                   Last_Error:
                 Skip_Counter: 0
          Exec_Master_Log_Pos: 770
              Relay_Log_Space: 243
              Until_Condition: None
               Until_Log_File:
                Until_Log_Pos: 0
           Master_SSL_Allowed: No
           Master_SSL_CA_File:
           Master_SSL_CA_Path:
              Master_SSL_Cert:
            Master_SSL_Cipher:
```

**Screen-shot 14—12: Show slave status command executed on replicating slave mobilestatisticsprofessor.com**

Execute *change master* command on Node 3 to establish replication from Node 2. Then, execute *start slave* on Node 3 to start replicating.

```
mysql> change master to master_host='mobilestatisticsprofessor.com', master_user
='repl', master_password='velcro20', master_log_file='mysql-bin.000001', master_
log_pos=98;
Query OK, 0 rows affected (0.37 sec)

mysql> start slave;
Query OK, 0 rows affected (0.03 sec)
```

**Screen-shot 14—13: Change master command issued on the slave ool-43524ec6.dyn.optonline.net  at end of the replication chain to replicate from slave mobilestatistcsprofessor.com**

Verify slave status on Node 3.  Slave I/O and SQL threads need to run without error for the slave to replicate from master successfully..  Additionally, *show processlist* command can be executed to verify processes running.

```
mysql> show slave status\G
*************************** 1. row ***************************
               Slave_IO_State: Waiting for master to send event
                  Master_Host: mobilestatisticsprofessor.com
                  Master_User: repl
                  Master_Port: 3306
                Connect_Retry: 60
              Master_Log_File: mysql-bin.000001
          Read_Master_Log_Pos: 98
               Relay_Log_File: mysql-relay-bin.000002
                Relay_Log_Pos: 244
        Relay_Master_Log_File: mysql-bin.000001
             Slave_IO_Running: Yes
            Slave_SQL_Running: Yes
              Replicate_Do_DB:
          Replicate_Ignore_DB:
           Replicate_Do_Table:
       Replicate_Ignore_Table:
      Replicate_Wild_Do_Table:
  Replicate_Wild_Ignore_Table:
                   Last_Errno: 0
                   Last_Error:
                 Skip_Counter: 0
          Exec_Master_Log_Pos: 98
              Relay_Log_Space: 400
              Until_Condition: None
               Until_Log_File:
                Until_Log_Pos: 0
           Master_SSL_Allowed: No
           Master_SSL_CA_File:
           Master_SSL_CA_Path:
              Master_SSL_Cert:
            Master_SSL_Cipher:
               Master_SSL_Key:
        Seconds_Behind_Master: 0
Master_SSL_Verify_Server_Cert: No
                Last_IO_Errno: 0
                Last_IO_Error:
               Last_SQL_Errno: 0
               Last_SQL_Error:
  Replicate_Ignore_Server_Ids:
             Master_Server_Id: 2
1 row in set (0.00 sec)
```

**Screen-shot 14—14: Show slave status command executed at the slave ool-43524ec6.dyn.optonline.net at the end of the replication chain**

## 14.5 Summary

This chapter demonstrated how to establish replication involving a master and a chain of slaves replicating from one another.

# 15 Establishing Master-Multiple Slave Replication

This chapter presents methods to use for establishing replication to multiple slaves from one master.

## 15.1 Purpose

The purpose of one master multiple slaves can be geographically distributed backup or reporting to be carried out from multiple locations.

## 15.2 Approach

This approach to establish replication one master to multiple slaves is as follows.

- Create replication user account on the master for each slave to replicate to
- Make configuration changes in master my.cnf file
  - Master
    - Assign unique server id
    - To turn binary logging on
    - Optionally assign log file name format and location
    - Optionally assign relay log file name format and location
  - Each slave
    - Assign unique server id
    - Optionally assign relay log file name format and location
    - Optionally turn read_only on
- Restart MySQL servers after configuration changes
- Record log file name and log position of the master
- Execute *change master* to command on each slave to read log from the master
- *Start slave* on each slave
- Verify whether replication slave is running on each slave
- Verify processlist on each server

## 15.3 Logical Architecture

Logical architecture diagram of a single master multiple slaves is presented below.

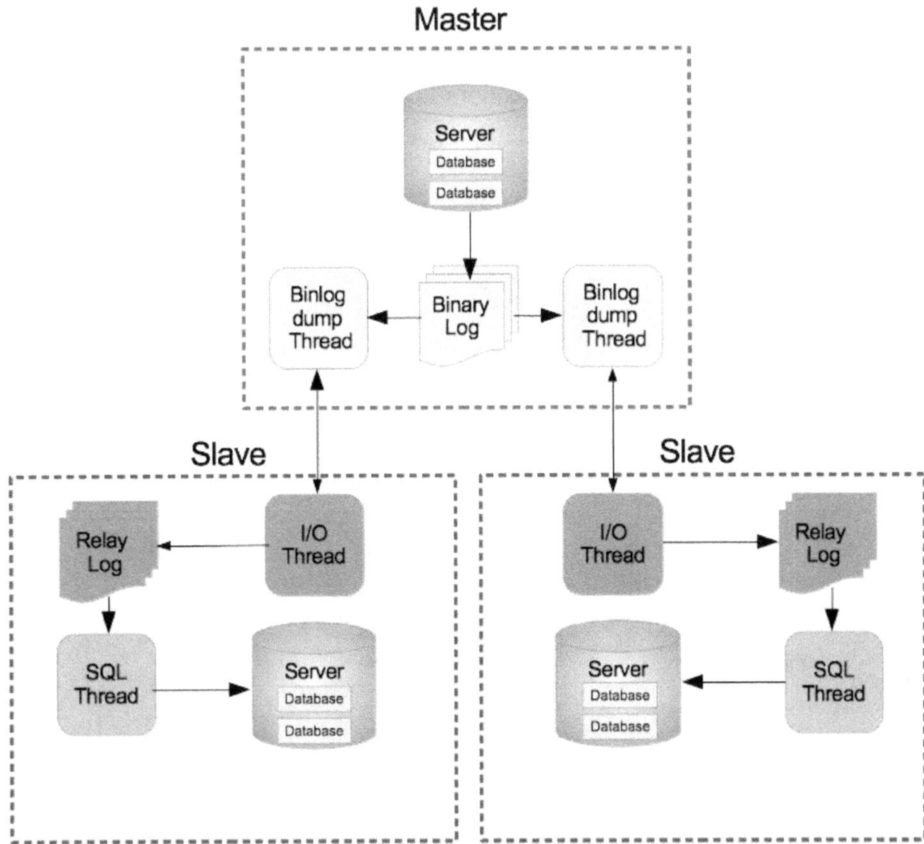


**Figure 15—1: Logical Architecture of a Master replicating to multiple Slaves**

## 15.4 Physical Architecture

Physical architecture diagram of one master and multiple slaves is presented below.

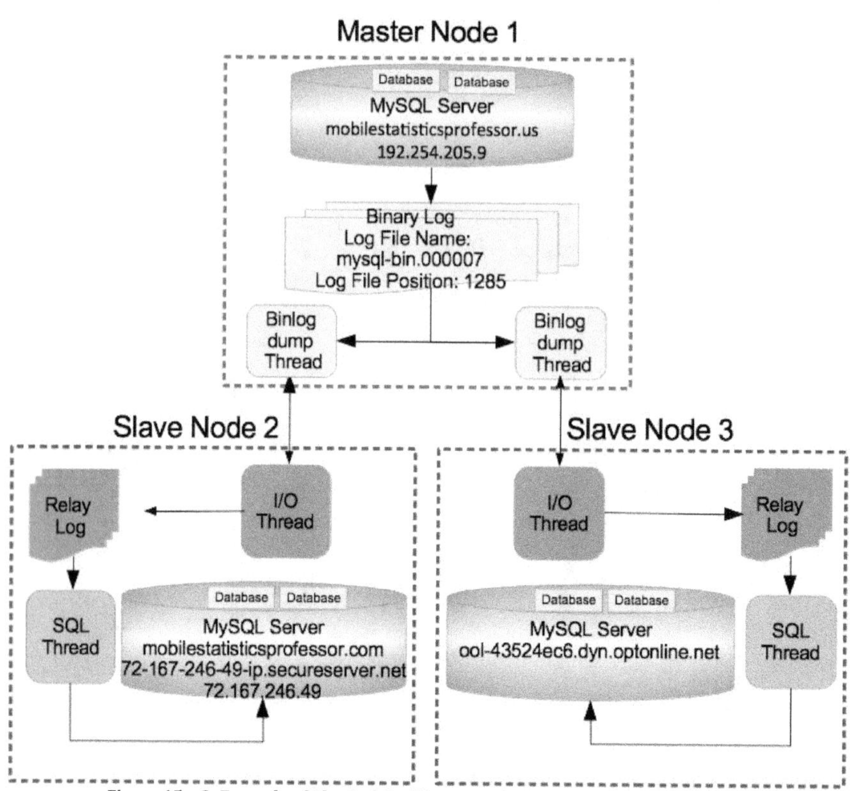


**Figure 15—2: Example of Physical Architecture of a Master replicating to multiple Slaves**

MySQL server host details are presented in the table below.

| Srl. No. | Node | Host/IP Address | server_id | Role |
|---|---|---|---|---|
| 1 | Node 1 | Mobilestatisticsprofessor.us, 192.254.205.9 | 1 | • Node 1 is master of Node 2 and Node 3 |
| 2 | Node 2 | Mobilestatisticsprofessor.com 72-167-246-49-ip.secureserver.net 72.167.246.49 | 2 | • Node 2 is slave of Node 1 |
| 3 | Node 2 | ool-43524ec6.dyn.optonline.net | 2 | • Node 3 is slave of Node 1 |

**Table 15—1: Single Master multiple Slaves MySQL Server Replication Configuration**

Create replication user account on Node 1 unless the replication accounts are already created. Create replication user account on Node 1 allowing Node 2 to read logs from Node 1. Execute *flush privileges* command if necessary.  Verify the grans to ensure that the replication user has at least *replication slave* grant. The choice of user id and password is up to the DBA to suit the organization's policies and standards.

Create replication user account on Node 1 allowing Node 2 to read logs from Node 1 and flush privileges.

```
mysql> grant replication slave, replication client on *.* to 'repl'@'mobilestati
sticsprofessor.com' identified by 'velcro20';
Query OK, 0 rows affected (0.00 sec)

mysql> flush privileges;
Query OK, 0 rows affected (0.00 sec)
```

**Screen-shot 15—1: Replication user for slave mobilestaticsprofessor.com is created on master mobilestatisticsprofessor.us**

Verify that the replication user created in Node 1 has required privileges to facilitate replication.

```
mysql> show grants for 'repl'@'mobilestatisticsprofessor.com'\G
*********************** 1. row ***********************
Grants for repl@mobilestatisticsprofessor.com: GRANT REPLICATION SLAVE, REPLICAT
ION CLIENT ON *.* TO 'repl'@'mobilestatisticsprofessor.com' IDENTIFIED BY PASSWO
RD '5373051f0cfcc009'
1 row in set (0.00 sec)
```

**Screen-shot 15—2: Verifying grants of replication user created on master mobilestatisticsprofessor.us**

Create replication user account on Node 1 allowing Node 3 to read logs from Node 1 and flush privileges.

```
mysql> grant replication client, replication slave on *.* to 'repl'@'ool-43524ec6.dyn.optonline.net' id
entified by 'velcro20';
Query OK, 0 rows affected (0.00 sec)

mysql> flush privileges;
Query OK, 0 rows affected (0.00 sec)
```

**Screen-shot 15—3: Replication user created on master mobilestatisticsprofessor.us for slave ool-43524ec6.dyn.optonline.net**

Verify that the replication user created in Node 1 has required privileges to facilitate replication.

```
mysql> show grants for 'repl'@'mobilestatisticsprofessor.com'\G
*************************** 1. row ***************************
Grants for repl@mobilestatisticsprofessor.com: GRANT REPLICATION SLAVE, REPLICAT
ION CLIENT ON *.* TO 'repl'@'mobilestatisticsprofessor.com' IDENTIFIED BY PASSWO
RD '5373051f0cfcc009'
1 row in set (0.00 sec)
```

**Screen-shot 15—4: Verifying grants on replication user on master mobilestatisticsprofessor.us for slave mobilestatisticsprofessor.com**

Make necessary configuration changes to the configuration file my.cnf located on Node 1. At a minimum, the following are added unless already present. Auto_increment_increment and auto_increment_offset can be set up to avoid collision of auto_increment key values among the MySQL servers participating in the replication configuration. server_id needs to be unique.  These are the minimum parameters, but these can be expanded to suit the particular need of the organization by the DBA.

*bin_log*
*server_id=1*

```
[mysqld]
local-infile=0
max_allowed_packet=16M
set-variable=local-infile=0
datadir=/var/lib/mysql
socket=/var/lib/mysql/mysql.sock
user=mysql
# Default to using old password format for compatibility with mysql 3.x
# clients (those using the mysqlclient10 compatibility package).
old_passwords=1

log_bin=/var/lib/mysql/mysql-bin.log
server_id=1
expire_logs_days=1
```

**Screen-shot 15—5: Excerpt of configuration file my.cnf from the master mobilestatisticsprofessor.us**

If my.cnf has been modified on Node 1, restart the MySQL server for the values to take effect.

```
[root@mob ~]# /etc/init.d/mysqld restart
Stopping MySQL:                                            [  OK  ]
Starting MySQL:                                            [  OK  ]
[root@mob ~]#
```

**Screen-shot 15—6: Restarted MySQL Server on master mobilestatisticsprofessor.us**

Make necessary configuration changes to the configuration file my.cnf located on Node 2. At a minimum, the following are added unless already present. Auto_increment_increment and auto_increment_offset can be set up to avoid collision of auto_increment key values among the MySQL servers participating in the replication configuration. server_id needs to be unique.  These are the minimum parameters, but these can be expanded to suit the particular need of the organization by the DBA. Excerpt of my.cnf file is not displayed here.

*server_id=2*

If my.cnf has been modified on Node 2, restart the MySQL server for the values to take effect. Output of restarting server is not displayed here.

Make necessary configuration changes to the configuration file my.cnf located on Node 3. At a minimum, the following are added unless already present. Auto_increment_increment and auto_increment_offset can be set up to avoid collision of auto_increment key values among the MySQL servers participating in the replication configuration. server_id needs to be unique.  These are the minimum parameters, but these can be expanded to suit the particular need of the organization by the DBA. Excerpt of my.cnf file is not displayed here.

*server_id=3*

If my.cnf has been modified on Node 3, restart the MySQL server for the values to take effect. Output of restarting server is not displayed here.

Record log file name and position on Node 1 by executing *show master status* command.

```
mysql> show master status\G
*************************** 1. row ***************************
             File: mysql-bin.000007
         Position: 1285
    Binlog_Do_DB:
Binlog_Ignore_DB:
1 row in set (0.00 sec)
```

**Screen-shot 15—7: Executed show master status on master mobilestatisticsprofessor.us**

Execute *change master* command on Node 2 to establish replication from Node 1. Then, execute *start slave* on Node 2 to start replicating.

```
mysql> change master to master_host='mobilestatisticsprofessor.us', master_user='repl', master_pa
ssword='velcro20', master_log_file='mysql-bin.000007', master_log_pos=1285;
Query OK, 0 rows affected (7.21 sec)

mysql> start slave;
Query OK, 0 rows affected (0.00 sec)
```

**Screen-shot 15—8: Change master command is issued on slave mobilestatisticsprofessor.com**

Execute *change master* command on Node 3 to establish replication from Node 1. Then, execute *start slave* on Node 3 to start replicating.

```
mysql> change master to master_host='mobilestatisticsprofessor.us', master_user=
'repl', master_log_file='mysql-bin.000007', master_log_pos=1285, master_password
='velcro20';
Query OK, 0 rows affected (0.23 sec)

mysql> start slave;
Query OK, 0 rows affected (0.00 sec)
```

Screen-shot 15—9: Change master command is executed on slave ool-43524ec6.dyn.optonline.net

Verify slave status on Node 2. Slave I/O and SQL threads need to run without error for the slave to replicate from master successfully. Additionally, *show processlist* command can be executed to verify processes running.

```
mysql> show slave status\G
*************************** 1. row ***************************
               Slave_IO_State: Waiting for master to send event
                  Master_Host: mobilestatisticsprofessor.us
                  Master_User: repl
                  Master_Port: 3306
                Connect_Retry: 60
              Master_Log_File: mysql-bin.000007
          Read_Master_Log_Pos: 1285
               Relay_Log_File: mysql-relay-bin.000002
                Relay_Log_Pos: 252
        Relay_Master_Log_File: mysql-bin.000007
             Slave_IO_Running: Yes
            Slave_SQL_Running: Yes
              Replicate_Do_DB:
          Replicate_Ignore_DB:
           Replicate_Do_Table:
       Replicate_Ignore_Table:
      Replicate_Wild_Do_Table:
  Replicate_Wild_Ignore_Table:
                   Last_Errno: 0
                   Last_Error:
                 Skip_Counter: 0
          Exec_Master_Log_Pos: 1285
              Relay_Log_Space: 408
              Until_Condition: None
               Until_Log_File:
                Until_Log_Pos: 0
           Master_SSL_Allowed: No
           Master_SSL_CA_File:
           Master_SSL_CA_Path:
              Master_SSL_Cert:
            Master_SSL_Cipher:
               Master_SSL_Key:
        Seconds_Behind_Master: 0
Master_SSL_Verify_Server_Cert: No
                Last_IO_Errno: 0
                Last_IO_Error:
               Last_SQL_Errno: 0
               Last_SQL_Error:
   Replicate_Ignore_Server_Ids:
             Master_Server_Id: 1
1 row in set (0.00 sec)
```

**Screen-shot 15—10: Show slave status command is executed on slave mobilestatisticsprofessor.com**

Similarly, verify slave status on Node 3. Slave I/O and SQL threads need to run without error for the slave to replicate from master successfully. Additionally, *show processlist* command can be executed to verify processes running.

One master server Node 1, *show processlist* command is be executed to verify processes running. The screenshot below displays that 2 *Binlog dump* threads are running since 2 slaves established Node 1 as master. Process id 62 corresponds to Node 2 and process id 65 corresponds to Node 3.

```
mysql> show processlist\G
*************************** 1. row ***************************
     Id: 61
   User: root
   Host: localhost
     db: NULL
Command: Query
   Time: 0
  State: NULL
   Info: show processlist
*************************** 2. row ***************************
     Id: 62
   User: repl
   Host: ip-72-167-246-49.ip.secureserver.net:51948
     db: NULL
Command: Binlog Dump
   Time: 1268
  State: Has sent all binlog to slave; waiting for binlog to be updated
   Info: NULL
*************************** 3. row ***************************
     Id: 65
   User: repl
   Host: ool-43524ec6.dyn.optonline.net:50082
     db: NULL
Command: Binlog Dump
   Time: 70
  State: Has sent all binlog to slave; waiting for binlog to be updated
   Info: NULL
3 rows in set (0.00 sec)
```

**Screen-shot 15—11: Show processlist command is executed on master mobilestatisticsprofessor.us**


## 15.5 Summary

This chapter demonstrated how to establish replication from a master to two slaves. The same mechanism can be used to extend replication to more than 2 slaves.

# 16 Establishing Master-Master-Master Circular Replication

This chapter describes the steps necessary to establish multi-master circular replication.

## 16.1 Purpose

The purpose of multi-master circular replication could be back up, fail-over or high availability.

## 16.2 Approach

Multi-master circular replication is established as follows.

- Create replication user account in each master for the server it replicate to.
- Make configuration changes in each master my.cnf file
    - Assign unique server id
    - To turn binary logging on
    - Optionally assign log file name format and location
    - Optionally assign relay log file name format and location
- Restart MySQL servers after configuration changes
- Record log file name and log position of each master
- Execute *change master* command on the slaves to replicate from respective masters
- Start slave on each master
- Verify whether replication slave is running on each master
- Verify *processlist* on each master

## 16.3  Logical Architecture

Three or more master MySQL servers can participate in circular replication from one master to another. A logical architecture of three-master circular replication is presented below.

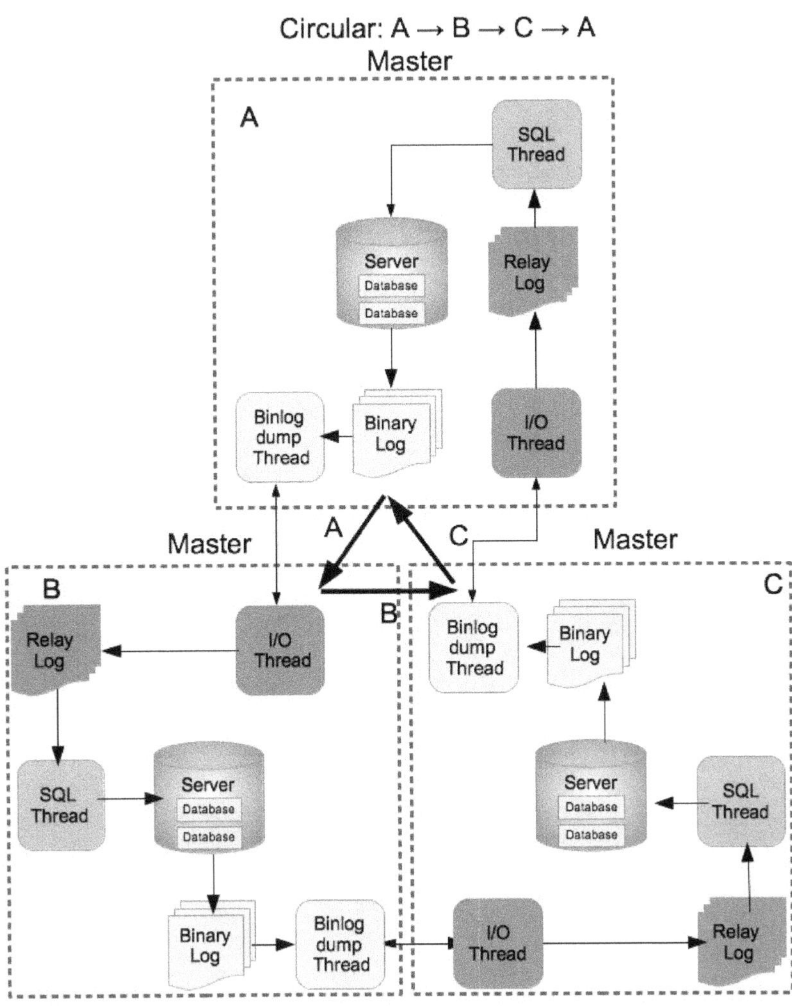


Figure 16—1: Logical Architecture of multi-master circular replication

103

## 16.4 Example of Physical Architecture

Physical architecture of master-master-master circular replication configuration is presented below.

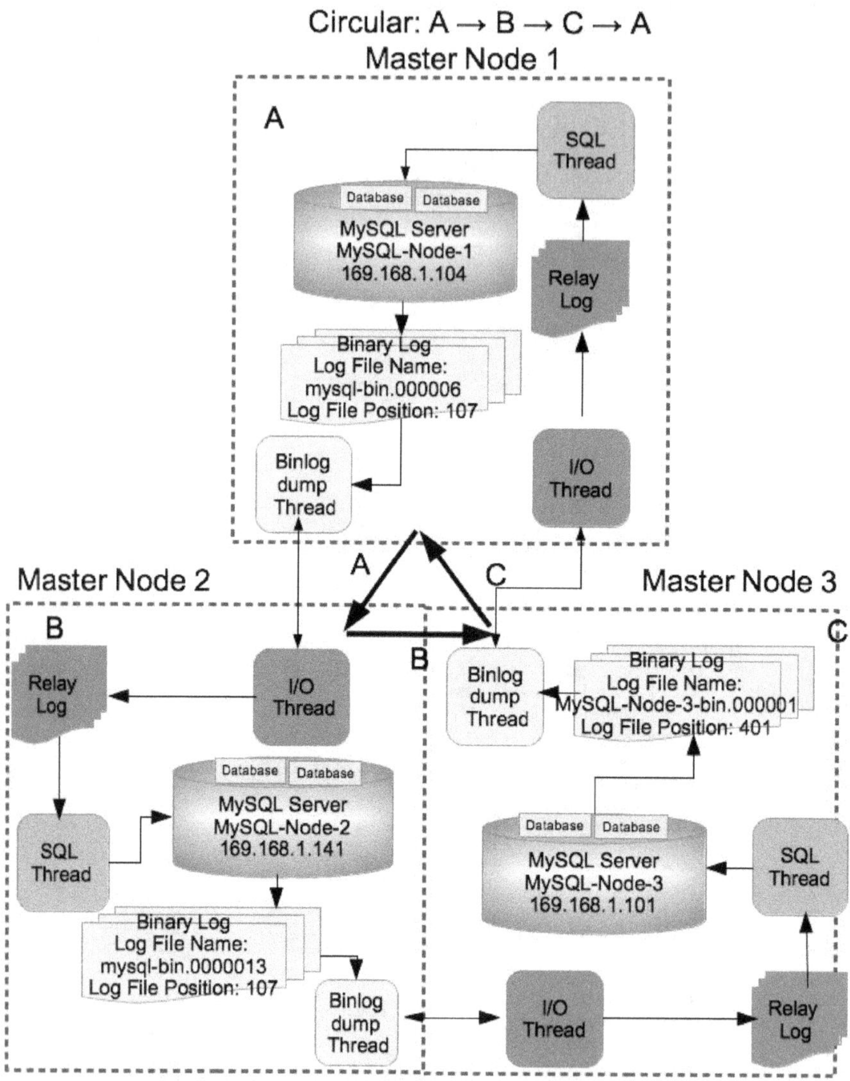


**Figure 16—2: Example of Physical Architecture of multi-master circular replication**

Three MySQL Servers located on a LAN. The roles of the servers and server IP address and hostnames are presented below.

| Srl. No. | Hostname | IP Address | server _id | Role |
|---|---|---|---|---|
| 1 | MySQL-Node-1 | 169.168.11.104 | 11 | • Master of MySQL-Node-2<br>• Slave of MySQL-Node-3 |
| 2 | MySQL-Node-2 | 169.168.1.141 | 10 | • Master of MySQL-Node-3<br>• Slave of MySQL-Node-1 |
| 3 | MySQL-Node-3 | 169.168.1.101 | 3000 | • Master of MySQL-Node-1<br>• Slave of MySQL-Node-2 |

Table 16—1: Master-Master-Master Circular Replication Host Configuration

## 16.5 Steps

Create replication users in each master to replicate to respective slaves. On MySQL-Node-1, create replication user for MySQL-Node-2. On MySQL-Node-2, create replication user for MySQL-Node-3. On MySQL-Node-3, create replication user for MySQL-Node-1. *Flush privileges* if necessary. Replication user id and password can be of the DBA's choice suiting the needs of the particular organization.

On MySQL-Node-1, create replication user for MySQL-Node-2.

```
mysql> grant replication slave, replication client on *.* to 'repl'@'MySQL-Node-
2' identified by 'velcro20';
Query OK, 0 rows affected (0.00 sec)
```
**Screen-shot 16—1: Create replication user to replicate to MySQL-Node-2**

On MySQL-Node-2, create replication user for MySQL-Node-3.

```
mysql> grant replication slave, replication client on *.* to 'repl'@'MySQL-Node-
3' identified by 'velcro20';
Query OK, 0 rows affected (0.00 sec)
```
**Screen-shot 16—2: Create replication user to replicate to MySQL-Node-3**

On MySQL-Node-3, create replication user for MySQL-Node-1.
```
mysql> grant replication slave, replication client on *.* to 'repl'@'MySQL-Node-
1' identified by 'velcro20';
Query OK, 0 rows affected (0.03 sec)
```
**Screen-shot 16—3: Create replication user to replicate to MySQL-Node-1**

Make configuration changes to facilitate replication unless the my.cnf files already contain parameters below to establish replication. These are minimum configurations. These parameters can be expanded and more parameters can be added as required by the replication configuration scenario.

On MySQL-Node-1, /etc/my.cnf, the following lines are added.

*server_id=11*
*log_bin*

On MySQL-Node-2, /etc/my.cnf, the following lines are added.

*server_id=10*
*log_bin*

On MySQL-Node-3, /etc/my.cnf, the following lines are added.

*server_id=3000*
*log_bin*

Restart the MySQL Server(s) if required to make the replication parameters to take effect.
*$/etc/init.d/mysqld restart*

On MySQL-Node-1, verify the binary logging status, hostname and server_id.

```
mysql> show variables like 'log_bin';
+---------------+-------+
| Variable_name | Value |
+---------------+-------+
| log_bin       | ON    |
+---------------+-------+
1 row in set (0.06 sec)

mysql> show variables like 'hostname';
+---------------+--------------+
| Variable_name | Value        |
+---------------+--------------+
| hostname      | MySQL-Node-1 |
+---------------+--------------+
1 row in set (0.00 sec)

mysql> show variables like 'server_id';
+---------------+-------+
| Variable_name | Value |
+---------------+-------+
| server_id     | 11    |
+---------------+-------+
1 row in set (0.01 sec)
```

**Screen-shot 16—4: log_bin, hostname and server_id variables are queried on master MySQL-Node-1**

Execute *show master status* command on MySQL-Node-3 to determine binary log coordinates.

```
mysql> show master status\G
*************************** 1. row ***************************
             File: MySQL-Node-3-bin.000001
         Position: 1338
     Binlog_Do_DB:
 Binlog_Ignore_DB:
Executed_Gtid_Set:
1 row in set (0.00 sec)
```

**Screen-shot 16—3: Show master status is executed on master MySQL-Node-3 (IP Address 169.168.1.101)**

Execute change master command on MySQL-Node-1 to replicate from master MySQL-Node-3 and start the slave.

```
mysql> change master to master_host='MySQL-Node-3', master_user='repl', master_p
assword='velcro20', master_log_file='MySQL-Node-3-bin.000001', master_log_pos=13
38;
Query OK, 0 rows affected (0.26 sec)

mysql> start slave;
Query OK, 0 rows affected (0.01 sec)
```

**Screen-shot 16—4: Change master and start slave commands executed on master My-SQL-Node-1 to replicate from master MySQL-Node-3 (IP Address 169.168.1.101)**

Verify slave status on MySQL-Node-1 by running *show slave status* command. In the screenshot below, both the Slave I/O and SQL threads are running without any error.

```
mysql> show slave status\G
*************************** 1. row ***************************
               Slave_IO_State: Waiting for master to send event
                  Master_Host: 169.168.1.101
                  Master_User: repl
                  Master_Port: 3306
                Connect_Retry: 60
              Master_Log_File: MySQL-Node-3-bin.000004
          Read_Master_Log_Pos: 1122
               Relay_Log_File: mysql-relay-bin.000002
                Relay_Log_Pos: 273
        Relay_Master_Log_File: MySQL-Node-3-bin.000004
             Slave_IO_Running: Yes
            Slave_SQL_Running: Yes
              Replicate_Do_DB:
          Replicate_Ignore_DB:
           Replicate_Do_Table:
       Replicate_Ignore_Table:
      Replicate_Wild_Do_Table:
  Replicate_Wild_Ignore_Table:
                   Last_Errno: 0
                   Last_Error:
                 Skip_Counter: 0
          Exec_Master_Log_Pos: 1122
              Relay_Log_Space: 429
              Until_Condition: None
               Until_Log_File:
                Until_Log_Pos: 0
           Master_SSL_Allowed: No
           Master_SSL_CA_File:
           Master_SSL_CA_Path:
              Master_SSL_Cert:
            Master_SSL_Cipher:
               Master_SSL_Key:
        Seconds_Behind_Master: 0
Master_SSL_Verify_Server_Cert: No
                Last_IO_Errno: 0
                Last_IO_Error:
               Last_SQL_Errno: 0
               Last_SQL_Error:
    Replicate_Ignore_Server_Ids:
             Master_Server_Id: 3000
1 row in set (0.12 sec)
```

**Screen-shot 16—5:** Show slave status command is executed in master MySQL-Node-1 replicating from master MySQL-Node-3 (IP Address 169.168.1.101). MySQL-Node-1 is a slave of MySQL-Node-3.

*Show processlist* command is execute on MySQL-Node-1. MySQL-Node-1 (slave) has processed master's binary log. MySQL-Node-1 has sent all the logs to slave MySQL-Node-2 as shown by the Binlog dump process.

```
mysql> show processlist\G
*********************** 1. row ***********************
     Id: 4
   User: ODBC
   Host: localhost:49801
     db: NULL
Command: Sleep
   Time: 52
  State:
   Info: NULL
*********************** 2. row ***********************
     Id: 18
   User: repl
   Host: MYSQL-NODE-2:49180
     db: NULL
Command: Binlog Dump
   Time: 2400
  State: Master has sent all binlog to slave; waiting for binlog to be updated
   Info: NULL
*********************** 3. row ***********************
     Id: 23
   User: root
   Host: MYSQL-NODE-2:49681
     db: NULL
Command: Query
   Time: 0
  State: NULL
   Info: show processlist
*********************** 4. row ***********************
     Id: 34
   User: system user
   Host:
     db: NULL
Command: Connect
   Time: 54
  State: Waiting for master to send event
   Info: NULL
*********************** 5. row ***********************
     Id: 35
   User: system user
   Host:
     db: NULL
Command: Connect
   Time: 53
  State: Slave has read all relay log; waiting for the slave I/O thread to updat
e it
   Info: NULL
5 rows in set (0.00 sec)
```

**Screen-shot 16—5: Show processlist command is executed on master MySQL-Node-1. MySQL-Node-1 is a slave of MySQL-Node-3 and master of MySQL-Node-2.**

On MySQL-Node-2, verify the binary logging status, hostname and server_id.

```
mysql> show variables like 'log_bin';
+---------------+-------+
| Variable_name | Value |
+---------------+-------+
| log_bin       | ON    |
+---------------+-------+
1 row in set (0.00 sec)

mysql> show variables like 'hostname';
+---------------+-------------+
| Variable_name | Value       |
+---------------+-------------+
| hostname      | MySQL-Node-2 |
+---------------+-------------+
1 row in set (0.00 sec)

mysql> show variables like 'server_id';
+---------------+-------+
| Variable_name | Value |
+---------------+-------+
| server_id     | 10    |
+---------------+-------+
1 row in set (0.00 sec)
```

Screen-shot 16—6: log_bin, hostname and server_id variables are queried on master MySQL-Node-2

Execute *show master status* command on MySQL-Node-1 to determine binary log coordinates.

```
mysql> show master status\G
*************************** 1. row ***************************
            File: mysql-bin.000006
        Position: 107
    Binlog_Do_DB:
Binlog_Ignore_DB:
1 row in set (0.20 sec)
```

Screen-shot 16—7: Show master status is executed on master MySQL-Node-1

Execute change master command on MySQL-Node-2 to replicate from master MySQL-Node-1 and start the slave.

```
mysql> change master to master_host='MySQL-Node-1', master_user='repl', master_p
assword='velcro20', master_log_file='mysql-bin-000006', master_log_pos=107;
Query OK, 0 rows affected (0.22 sec)

mysql> start slave;
Query OK, 0 rows affected (0.01 sec)
```

Screen-shot 16—8: Change master command is executed on master piyush-HP to replicate from master Mac-Mini.local. piyush-HP is a slave of Mac-Mini.local

Verify slave status on MySQL-Node-2 by running *show slave status* command. In the screen-shot below, both the Slave I/O and SQL threads are running without any error.

```
mysql> show slave status\G
*************************** 1. row ***************************
               Slave_IO_State: Waiting for master to send event
                  Master_Host: MySQL-Node-1
                  Master_User: repl
                  Master_Port: 3306
                Connect_Retry: 60
              Master_Log_File: mysql-bin.000006
          Read_Master_Log_Pos: 107
               Relay_Log_File: mysql-relay-bin.000002
                Relay_Log_Pos: 253
        Relay_Master_Log_File: mysql-bin.000006
             Slave_IO_Running: Yes
            Slave_SQL_Running: Yes
              Replicate_Do_DB:
          Replicate_Ignore_DB:
           Replicate_Do_Table:
       Replicate_Ignore_Table:
      Replicate_Wild_Do_Table:
  Replicate_Wild_Ignore_Table:
                   Last_Errno: 0
                   Last_Error:
                 Skip_Counter: 0
          Exec_Master_Log_Pos: 107
              Relay_Log_Space: 409
              Until_Condition: None
               Until_Log_File:
                Until_Log_Pos: 0
           Master_SSL_Allowed: No
           Master_SSL_CA_File:
           Master_SSL_CA_Path:
              Master_SSL_Cert:
            Master_SSL_Cipher:
               Master_SSL_Key:
        Seconds_Behind_Master: 0
Master_SSL_Verify_Server_Cert: No
                Last_IO_Errno: 0
                Last_IO_Error:
               Last_SQL_Errno: 0
               Last_SQL_Error:
  Replicate_Ignore_Server_Ids:
             Master_Server_Id: 11
1 row in set (0.00 sec)
```

**Screen-shot 16—9: Show slave status executed in master MySQL-Node-2 that is slave of master MySQL-Node-1.**

*Show processlist* command is execute on MySQL-Node-2. MySQL-Node-2 (slave) has processed master's binary log. MySQL-Node-2 has sent all the logs to slave MySQL-Node-3 as shown by the Binlog dump process.

```
mysql> show processlist\G
*********************** 1. row ***********************
     Id: 1
   User: system user
   Host:
     db: NULL
Command: Connect
   Time: 2465
  State: Slave has read all relay log; waiting for the slave I/O thread to updat
e it
   Info: NULL
*********************** 2. row ***********************
     Id: 2
   User: system user
   Host:
     db: NULL
Command: Connect
   Time: 2516
  State: Waiting for master to send event
   Info: NULL
*********************** 3. row ***********************
     Id: 6
   User: root
   Host: MySQL-Node-2:49617
     db: NULL
Command: Query
   Time: 0
  State: NULL
   Info: show processlist
*********************** 4. row ***********************
     Id: 7
   User: repl
   Host: MySQL-Node-3:49192
     db: NULL
Command: Binlog Dump
   Time: 884
  State: Master has sent all binlog to slave; waiting for binlog to be updated
   Info: NULL
4 rows in set (0.00 sec)
```

Screen-shot 16—10: Show processlist executed and hostname queried on MySQL-Node-2. MySQL-Node-2 is the master of MySQL-Node-3 and slave of MySQL-Node-1.

On MySQL-Node-1, verify the binary logging status, hostname and server_id.

```
mysql> show variables like 'log_bin';
+---------------+-------+
| Variable_name | Value |
+---------------+-------+
| log_bin       | ON    |
+---------------+-------+
1 row in set (0.77 sec)

mysql> show variables like 'hostname';
+---------------+--------------+
| Variable_name | Value        |
+---------------+--------------+
| hostname      | MySQL-Node-3 |
+---------------+--------------+
1 row in set (0.01 sec)

mysql> show variables like 'server_id';
+---------------+-------+
| Variable_name | Value |
+---------------+-------+
| server_id     | 3000  |
+---------------+-------+
1 row in set (0.01 sec)
```

Screen-shot 16—11: log_bin, hostname and server_id variables are queried on master host MySQL-Node-3

Execute *show master status* command on MySQL-Node-2 to determine binary log coordinates.

```
mysql> show master status\G
*************************** 1. row ***************************
            File: mysql-bin.000013
        Position: 107
    Binlog_Do_DB:
Binlog_Ignore_DB:
1 row in set (0.00 sec)
```

**Screen-shot 16—12: Show master status is executed on master MySQL-Node-2**

Execute change master command on MySQL-Node-3 to replicate from master MySQL-Node-2 and start the slave.

```
mysql> change master to master_host='MySQL-Node-2', master_user='repl', master_p
assword='velcro20', master_log_file='mysql-bin.000013', master_log_pos=107;
Query OK, 0 rows affected, 2 warnings (0.55 sec)

mysql> start slave;
Query OK, 0 rows affected (0.22 sec)
```

**Screen-shot 16—13: Change master command executed on master MySQL-Node-3 to replicate from master MySQL-Node-2. MySQL-Node-3 becomes a slave of MySQL-Node-2.**

Verify slave status on MySQL-Node-3 by running *show slave status* command. In the screen-shot below, both the Slave I/O and SQL threads are running without any error.

```
mysql> show slave status\G
*********************** 1. row ***********************
               Slave_IO_State: Waiting for master to send event
                  Master_Host: MySQL-Node-2
                  Master_User: repl
                  Master_Port: 3306
                Connect_Retry: 60
              Master_Log_File: mysql-bin.000015
          Read_Master_Log_Pos: 107
               Relay_Log_File: MySQL-Node-3-relay-bin.000010
                Relay_Log_Pos: 266
        Relay_Master_Log_File: mysql-bin.000015
             Slave_IO_Running: Yes
            Slave_SQL_Running: Yes
              Replicate_Do_DB:
          Replicate_Ignore_DB:
           Replicate_Do_Table:
       Replicate_Ignore_Table:
      Replicate_Wild_Do_Table:
  Replicate_Wild_Ignore_Table:
                   Last_Errno: 0
                   Last_Error:
                 Skip_Counter: 0
          Exec_Master_Log_Pos: 107
              Relay_Log_Space: 588
              Until_Condition: None
               Until_Log_File:
                Until_Log_Pos: 0
           Master_SSL_Allowed: No
           Master_SSL_CA_File:
           Master_SSL_CA_Path:
              Master_SSL_Cert:
            Master_SSL_Cipher:
               Master_SSL_Key:
        Seconds_Behind_Master: 0
Master_SSL_Verify_Server_Cert: No
                Last_IO_Errno: 0
                Last_IO_Error:
               Last_SQL_Errno: 0
               Last_SQL_Error:
  Replicate_Ignore_Server_Ids:
             Master_Server_Id: 10
                  Master_UUID:
             Master_Info_File: c:\mysql-5.6.17-win32\data\master.info
                    SQL_Delay: 0
          SQL_Remaining_Delay: NULL
      Slave_SQL_Running_State: Slave has read all relay log; waiting for the sla
ve I/O thread to update it
           Master_Retry_Count: 86400
                  Master_Bind:
      Last_IO_Error_Timestamp:
     Last_SQL_Error_Timestamp:
               Master_SSL_Crl:
           Master_SSL_Crlpath:
           Retrieved_Gtid_Set:
            Executed_Gtid_Set:
                Auto_Position: 0
1 row in set (0.66 sec)
```

**Screen-shot 16—14: Show slave status is executed on MySQL-Node-3 (IP Address 169.168.1.101)**

*Show processlist* command is execute on MySQL-Node-3. MySQL-Node-3 (slave) has processed master's binary log. MySQL-Node-3 has sent all the logs to slave MySQL-Node-1 as shown by the Binlog dump process.

```
mysql> show processlist\G
*************************** 1. row ***************************
     Id: 1
   User: system user
   Host:
     db: NULL
Command: Connect
   Time: 977
  State: Waiting for master to send event
   Info: NULL
*************************** 2. row ***************************
     Id: 2
   User: system user
   Host:
     db: NULL
Command: Connect
   Time: 934
  State: Slave has read all relay log; waiting for the slave I/O thread to updat
e it
   Info: NULL
*************************** 3. row ***************************
     Id: 5
   User: root
   Host: MySQL-Node-2:49664
     db: NULL
Command: Query
   Time: 0
  State: init
   Info: show processlist
*************************** 4. row ***************************
     Id: 12
   User: root
   Host: localhost:49212
     db: NULL
Command: Sleep
   Time: 241
  State:
   Info: NULL
*************************** 5. row ***************************
     Id: 19
   User: repl
   Host: MySQL-Node-1:50825
     db: NULL
Command: Binlog Dump
   Time: 169
  State: Master has sent all binlog to slave; waiting for binlog to be updated
   Info: NULL
5 rows in set (0.01 sec)
```

Screen-shot 16—15: Show processlist command is executed and hostname is queried on master MySQL-Node-3. Master MySQL-Node-3 is the master of MySQL-Node-1 and slave of MySQL-Node-2

## 16.6 Summary

This chapter provided the steps with examples to establish circular replication among multiple masters.

# 17 Establishing Master-Master-Slave-Slave Replication

This chapter presents how to establish bi-directional replication between two masters. Then, extend the configuration to enable each master to replicate to one or more slaves.

## 17.1 Purpose

The purpose of master-master-slave-slave type of replication can be to accomplish failover, high availability, backup as well as reporting.


## 17.2 Approach


- Create replication user account in each master for the other master and each slave to replicate to.
- Make configuration changes in my.cnf file
  - Master
    - Assign unique server id
    - To turn binary logging on
    - Optionally assign log file name format and location
    - Optionally assign relay log file name format and location
    - Set auto_increment_increment and auto_increment_offset on
  - Slave
    - Assign unique server id
    - Optionally assign relay log file name format and location
    - Optionally, set auto_increment_increment and auto_increment_offset on
- Restart MySQL servers after configuration changes
- Record log file name and log position from each master
- Execute change master to command
  - on each master to replicate from the other master
  - on each slave to replicate from the master.
- Start slave on each master and slave
- Verify whether replication slave is running on master and slave servers
- Verify process list on each server

## 17.3  Logical Architecture

Logical architecture of master-master-slave-slave replication configuration is presented below.

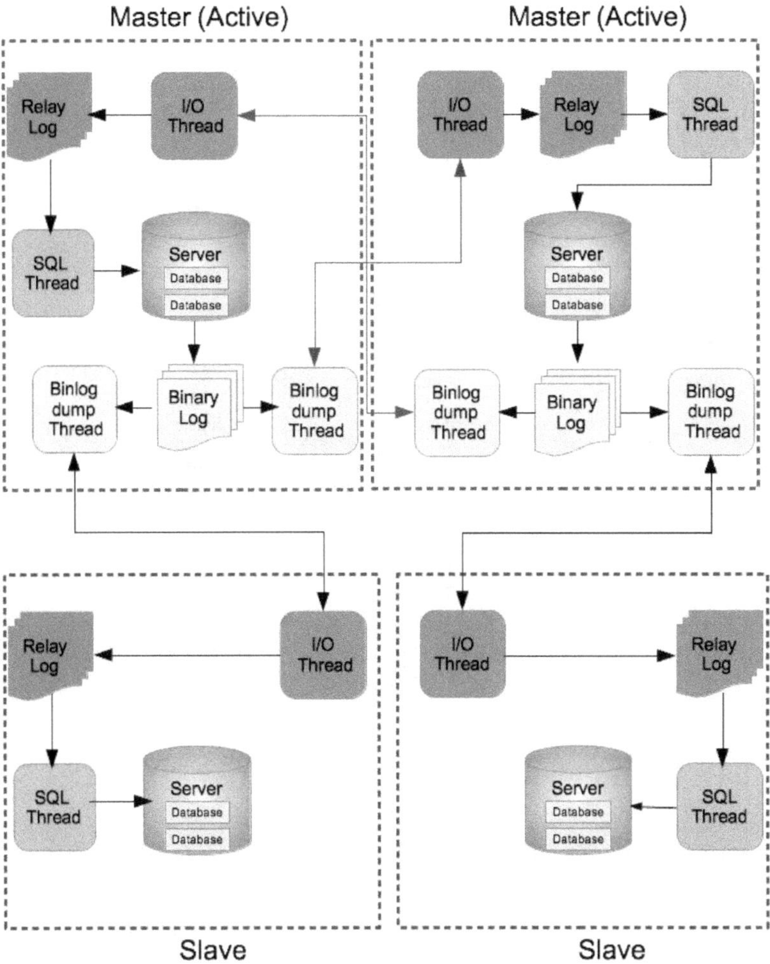


Figure 17—1: Logical Architecture of Master-Master replication where each master replicates to its own slave

## 17.4  Physical Architecture

Physical architecture of master-master-slave-slave replication configuration is presented below.

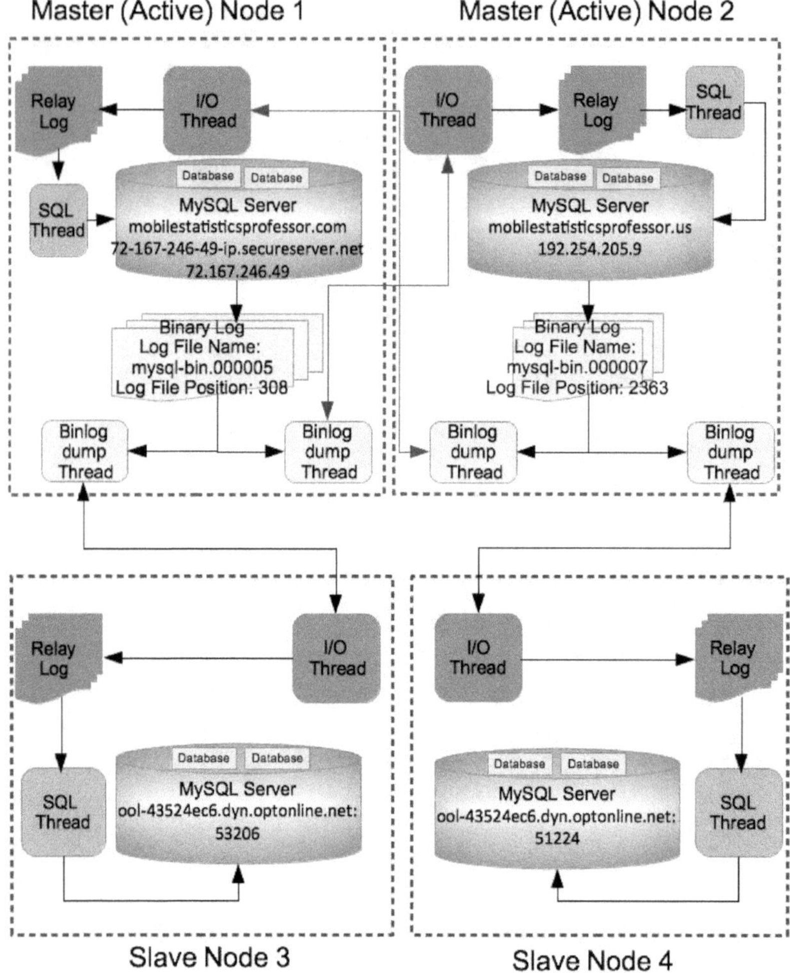


Figure 17—2: Example of Physical Architecture of Master-Master replication where each Master is replicating to its own Slave

118

Four MySQL Servers are participating in the master-master-slave-slave configuration. Node 1 and 2 are masters. Bi-directional replication is established between them, Node is a slave of Node 1 and Node 4 is a slave of Node 2.

| Srl. No. | Node | IP Address | Role |
|---|---|---|---|
| 1 | Node 1 | Mobilestatisticsprofessor.us, 192.254.205.9 | • Master of Node 2<br>• Master of Node 3 |
| 2 | Node 2 | Mobilestatisticsprofessor.com 72-167-246-49-ip.secureserver.net 72.167.246.49 | • Master of Node 1<br>• Master of Node 4 |
| 3 | Node 2 | ool-43524ec6.dyn.optonline.net:53206 | • Slave of Node 1 |
| 4 | Node 4 | ool-43524ec6.dyn.optonline.net: 51224 | • Slave of Node 2 |

**Table 17—1: Master-Master-Slave-Slave Replication Configuration**

## 17.5 Steps

Create replication user account on Node 1 unless the replication accounts are already created. Create replication user account on Node 1 allowing Node 2 to read logs from Node 1. Create the mirror image account on Node 2 for Node 1 to replicate. Create account on Node 1 for Node 3 to replicate. Create user account on Node 3 to replicate to Node 4. Execute *flush privileges* command if necessary. Verify the grans to ensure that the replication user has at least *replication slave* grant. The choice of user id and password is up to the DBA to suit the organization's policies and standards.

Create replication user account on Node 1 allowing Node 2 to read logs from Node 1 and flush privileges.

```
mysql> grant replication slave, replication client on *.* to 'repl'@'mobilestati
sticsprofessor.us' identified by 'velcro20';
Query OK, 0 rows affected (0.00 sec)

mysql> flush privileges;
Query OK, 0 rows affected (0.00 sec)
```

**Screen-shot 17—1: Added replication user to master mobilestatisticsprofessor.com**

Verify that the replication user created in Node 1 has required privileges to facilitate replication.

```
mysql> show grants for 'repl'@'mobilestatisticsprofessor.us'\G
*************************** 1. row ***************************
Grants for repl@mobilestatisticsprofessor.us: GRANT REPLICATION SLAVE, REPLICATI
ON CLIENT ON *.* TO 'repl'@'mobilestatisticsprofessor.us' IDENTIFIED BY PASSWORD
 '5373051f0cfcc009'
1 row in set (0.00 sec)
```

**Screen-shot 17—2: Verifying the replication user account on master mobilestatisticsprofessor.com**

Create replication user account on Node 1 allowing Node 3 to read logs from Node 1 and flush privileges.

```
mysql>  grant replication client, replication slave on *.* to 'repl'@'ool-43524ec6.dyn.optonline.net' id
entified by 'velcro20';
Query OK, 0 rows affected (0.00 sec)

mysql> flush privileges;
Query OK, 0 rows affected (0.00 sec)
```

**Screen-shot 17—3: Replication user created on master mobilestatisticsprofessor.us for slave ool-43524ec6.dyn.optonline.net**

Verify that the replication user created in Node 1 has required privileges to facilitate replication.

```
mysql> show grants for 'repl'@'ool-43524ec6.dyn.optonline.net'\G
*************************** 1. row ***************************
Grants for repl@ool-43524ec6.dyn.optonline.net: GRANT REPLICATION SLAVE, REPLICA
TION CLIENT ON *.* TO 'repl'@'ool-43524ec6.dyn.optonline.net' IDENTIFIED BY PASS
WORD '5373051f0cfcc009'
1 row in set (0.00 sec)
```

**Screen-shot 17—4: Verifying the replication user account on master mobilestatisticsprofessor.com**

Create replication user account on Node 2 allowing Node 1 to read logs from Node 2 and flush privileges.

```
mysql> show grants for 'repl'@'mobilestatisticsprofessor.com'\G
*************************** 1. row ***************************
Grants for repl@mobilestatisticsprofessor.com: GRANT REPLICATION SLAVE, REPLICAT
ION CLIENT ON *.* TO 'repl'@'mobilestatisticsprofessor.com' IDENTIFIED BY PASSWO
RD '5373051f0cfcc009'
1 row in set (0.00 sec)
```

**Screen-shot 17—5: Verifying grants of replication user created on master mobilestatisticsprofessor.us**

Create replication user account on Node 2 allowing Node 1 to read logs from Node 2 and flush privileges.

```
mysql> grant replication slave, replication client on *.* to 'repl'@'mobilestati
sticsprofessor.com' identified by 'velcro20';
Query OK, 0 rows affected (0.00 sec)

mysql> flush privileges;
Query OK, 0 rows affected (0.00 sec)
```

**Screen-shot 17—6: Replication user for slave mobilestaticsprofessor.com is created on master mobilestatisticsprofessor.us**

Verify that the replication user created in Node 2 has required privileges to facilitate replication.

```
mysql> show grants for 'repl'@'mobilestatisticsprofessor.com'\G
*************************** 1. row ***************************
Grants for repl@mobilestatisticsprofessor.com: GRANT REPLICATION SLAVE, REPLICAT
ION CLIENT ON *.* TO 'repl'@'mobilestatisticsprofessor.com' IDENTIFIED BY PASSWO
RD '5373051f0cfcc009'
1 row in set (0.00 sec)
```

**Screen-shot 17—7: Verifying grants on replication user on master mobilestatisticsprofessor.us for slave mobilestatisticsprofessor.com**

Create replication user account on Node 2 allowing Node 4 to read logs from Node 2 and flush privileges.

```
mysql>  grant replication client, replication slave on *.* to 'repl'@'ool-43524ec6.dyn.optonline.net' id
entified by 'velcro20';
Query OK, 0 rows affected (0.00 sec)

mysql> flush privileges;
Query OK, 0 rows affected (0.00 sec)
```

**Screen-shot 17—8: Replication user created on master mobilestatisticsprofessor.com for slave ool-43524ec6.dyn.optonline.net**

Verify that the replication user created in Node 2 has required privileges to facilitate replication.

```
mysql> show grants for 'repl'@'ool-43524ec6.dyn.optonline.net'\G
*************************** 1. row ***************************
Grants for repl@ool-43524ec6.dyn.optonline.net: GRANT REPLICATION SLAVE, REPLICA
TION CLIENT ON *.* TO 'repl'@'ool-43524ec6.dyn.optonline.net' IDENTIFIED BY PASS
WORD '5373051f0cfcc009'
1 row in set (0.00 sec)
```

**Screen-shot 17—9; Verifying the user account created on master mobilestatisticsprofessor.com**

Make necessary configuration changes to the configuration file my.cnf located on Node 1. At a minimum, the following are added unless already present. Auto_increment_increment and auto_increment_offset is set up to avoid collision of auto_increment key values among the MySQL servers participating in the replication configuration. server_id needs to be unique.  These are the minimum parameters, but these can be expanded to suit the particular need of the organization by the DBA.

*bin_log*
*server_id=1*
*auto_increment_increment=3*

Make necessary configuration changes to the configuration file my.cnf located on Node 1. At a minimum, the following are added unless already present. Auto_increment_increment and auto_increment_offset can be set up to avoid collision of auto_increment key values among the MySQL servers participating in the replication configuration. server_id needs to be unique.  These are the minimum parameters, but these can be expanded to suit the particular need of the organization by the DBA.

*bin_log*
*server_id=1*
*auto_increment_increment=3*
*auto_increment_offset=1*

```
[mysqld]
local-infile=0
max_allowed_packet=16M
set-variable=local-infile=0
datadir=/var/lib/mysql
socket=/var/lib/mysql/mysql.sock
user=mysql
# Default to using old password format for compatibility with mysql 3.x
# clients (those using the mysqlclient10 compatibility package).
old_passwords=1

log_bin=/var/lib/mysql/mysql-bin.log
server_id=1
expire_logs_days=1
```
**Screen-shot 17—10: Excerpt of configuration file my.cnf from the master mobilestatisticsprofessor.us**

If my.cnf has been modified on Node 1, restart the MySQL server for the values to take effect.

```
[root@mob ~]# /etc/init.d/mysqld restart
Stopping MySQL:                                    [  OK  ]
Starting MySQL:                                    [  OK  ]
[root@mob ~]#
```
**Screen-shot 17—11: Restarted MySQL Server on master mobilestatisticsprofessor.us**

Make necessary configuration changes to the configuration file my.cnf located on Node 2. At a minimum, the following are added unless already present. Auto_increment_increment and auto_increment_offset is set up to avoid collision of auto_increment key values among the MySQL servers participating in the replication configuration. server_id needs to be unique.  These are the minimum parameters, but these can be expanded to suit the particular need of the organization by the DBA.

*bin_log*
*server_id=2*
*auto_increment_increment=3*
*auto_increment_offset=2*

```
[mysqld]
datadir=/var/lib/mysql
socket=/var/lib/mysql/mysql.sock
user=mysql
# Default to using old password format for compatibility with mysql 3.x
# clients (those using the mysqlclient10 compatibility package).
old_passwords=1

#log_bin=/var/lib/mysql/mysql-bin.log
#relay_log=/var/lib/mysql/mysqld-relay-bin.log
#log_slave_updates
server_id=2
expire_logs_days=1
#read_only=1
auto_increment_increment=3
auto_increment_offset=2

[mysqld_safe]
log-error=/var/log/mysqld.log
pid-file=/var/run/mysqld/mysqld.pid
```

**Screen-shot 17—12: Configuration changes in master mobilestatisticsprofessor.com my.cnf file to support replication**

If my.cnf has been modified, restart the MySQL server for the values to take effect.

*$/etc/init.d/mysqld restart*

```
[root@ip-72-167-246-49 ~]# /etc/init.d/mysqld restart
Stopping MySQL:                                            [  OK  ]
Starting MySQL:                                            [  OK  ]
[root@ip-72-167-246-49 ~]#
```

**Screen-shot 17—13: Restarted MySQL server on master mobilestatisticsprofessor.com**

Verify log_bin, auto_increment_increment and auto_increment_offset parameters after the server is restarted to ensure that the parameters have been set correctly in Node 1.

```
mysql> show variables like 'log_bin';
+---------------+-------+
| Variable_name | Value |
+---------------+-------+
| log_bin       | ON    |
+---------------+-------+
1 row in set (0.00 sec)

mysql> show variables like 'server_id';
+---------------+-------+
| Variable_name | Value |
+---------------+-------+
| server_id     | 2     |
+---------------+-------+
1 row in set (0.00 sec)

mysql> show variables like 'auto_increment_increment';
+--------------------------+-------+
| Variable_name            | Value |
+--------------------------+-------+
| auto_increment_increment | 3     |
+--------------------------+-------+
1 row in set (0.00 sec)

mysql> show variables like 'auto_increment_offset';
+-----------------------+-------+
| Variable_name         | Value |
+-----------------------+-------+
| auto_increment_offset | 2     |
+-----------------------+-------+
1 row in set (0.00 sec)
```

**Screen-shot 17—14: Checking the log_bin, server_id, auto_increment_increment and auto_increment_offset variables in master mobilestatisticsprofessor.com**

Make necessary configuration changes to the configuration file my.cnf located on Node 3. At a minimum, the following is added unless already present. Auto_increment_increment and auto_increment_offset is set up to avoid collision of auto_increment key values among the MySQL servers participating in the replication configuration. server_id needs to be unique.  Read_only can be set for slave if desired.  Restart the server to make the changes take effect. These are the minimum parameters, but these can be expanded to suit the particular need of the organization by the DBA.

*server_id=3*

Make necessary configuration changes to the configuration file my.cnf located on Node 4. At a minimum, the following is added unless already present. Auto_increment_increment and auto_increment_offset is set up to avoid collision of auto_increment key values among the MySQL servers participating in the replication configuration. server_id needs to be unique.  Read_only can be set for slave if desired.  Restart the server to make the changes take effect. These are the minimum parameters, but these can be expanded to suit the particular need of the organization by the DBA.

*server_id=4*

Execute *show master status* command on Node 2 to determine binary log coordinates.

```
mysql> show master status\G
*************************** 1. row ***************************
            File: mysql-bin.000007
        Position: 2363
    Binlog_Do_DB:
Binlog_Ignore_DB:
1 row in set (0.00 sec)
```
**Screen-shot 17—15: Show master status command is executed on master mobilestatisticsprofessor.us**

Execute change master command on Node 1 to replicate from master Node 2 and start the slave.

```
mysql> change master to master_host='mobilestatisticsprofessor.us', master_user=
'repl', master_password='velcro20', master_log_file='mysql-bin.000007', master_l
og_pos=2363
    -> ;
Query OK, 0 rows affected (0.16 sec)

mysql> start slave;
Query OK, 0 rows affected (0.00 sec)
```
**Screen-shot 17—16: Change master command issued on master host mobilestatisticsprofesor.com to replicate from master host mobilestatisticsprofessor.us**

Verify slave status on Node 1 by running *show slave status* command. In the screen-shot below, both the Slave I/O and SQL threads are running without any error.

```
mysql> show slave status\G
*************************** 1. row ***************************
               Slave_IO_State: Waiting for master to send event
                  Master_Host: mobilestatisticsprofessor.us
                  Master_User: repl
                  Master_Port: 3306
                Connect_Retry: 60
              Master_Log_File: mysql-bin.000007
          Read_Master_Log_Pos: 2363
               Relay_Log_File: mysqld-relay-bin.000002
                Relay_Log_Pos: 243
        Relay_Master_Log_File: mysql-bin.000007
             Slave_IO_Running: Yes
            Slave_SQL_Running: Yes
              Replicate_Do_DB:
          Replicate_Ignore_DB:
           Replicate_Do_Table:
       Replicate_Ignore_Table:
      Replicate_Wild_Do_Table:
  Replicate_Wild_Ignore_Table:
                   Last_Errno: 0
                   Last_Error:
                 Skip_Counter: 0
          Exec_Master_Log_Pos: 2363
              Relay_Log_Space: 243
              Until_Condition: None
               Until_Log_File:
                Until_Log_Pos: 0
           Master_SSL_Allowed: No
           Master_SSL_CA_File:
           Master_SSL_CA_Path:
              Master_SSL_Cert:
            Master_SSL_Cipher:
               Master_SSL_Key:
        Seconds_Behind_Master: 0
1 row in set (0.00 sec)
```

**Screen-shot 17—17: Show slave status command is executed on master host mobilestatisticsprofessor.com. mobilestatisticsprofessor.com is a slave of mobilestatisticsprofessor.us.**

Verify processes running on Node by executing *show processlist* command. On Node 1.

```
*************************** 1. row ***************************
     Id: 26
   User: repl
   Host: ool-43524ec6.dyn.optonline.net:51623
     db: NULL
Command: Binlog Dump
   Time: 48006
  State: Has sent all binlog to slave; waiting for binlog to be updated
   Info: NULL
*************************** 2. row ***************************
     Id: 352
   User: repl
   Host: 192.254.205.8:56137
     db: NULL
Command: Binlog Dump
   Time: 612
  State: Has sent all binlog to slave; waiting for binlog to be updated
   Info: NULL
*************************** 3. row ***************************
     Id: 366
   User: root
   Host: localhost
     db: NULL
Command: Query
   Time: 0
  State: NULL
   Info: show processlist
*************************** 4. row ***************************
     Id: 370
   User: system user
   Host:
     db: NULL
Command: Connect
   Time: 39
  State: Waiting for master to send event
   Info: NULL
*************************** 5. row ***************************
     Id: 371
   User: system user
   Host:
     db: NULL
Command: Connect
   Time: 38
  State: Has read all relay log; waiting for the slave I/O thread to update it
   Info: NULL
5 rows in set (0.00 sec)
```

**Screen-shot 17—18:** Show processlist command is executed on mater mobilesatisticsprofessor.com that is also a slave of mobilestatisticsprofessor.us.

Execute *show master status* command on Node 1 to determine binary log coordinates.

```
mysql> show master status;
+--------------------+----------+--------------+------------------+
| File               | Position | Binlog_Do_DB | Binlog_Ignore_DB |
+--------------------+----------+--------------+------------------+
| mysql-bin.000005   |      308 |              |                  |
+--------------------+----------+--------------+------------------+
1 row in set (0.00 sec)
```

Screen-shot 17—19: Show master status command executed on master mobilestatisticsprofessor.com

Execute change master command on Node 2 to replicate from master Node 1 and start the slave.

```
mysql> change master to master_host='mobilestatisticsprofessor.com', master_user
='repl', master_password='velcro20', master_log_file='mysql-bin.000005', master_
log_pos=308;
Query OK, 0 rows affected (0.03 sec)

mysql> start slave;
Query OK, 0 rows affected (0.00 sec)
```

Screen-shot 17—20: Change maser command executed on master mobilestatisticsprofessor.us and slave is started. Mobilestatisticsprofesor.us becomes a slave of mobilestatisticsprofessor.com.

Verify slave status on Node 2 by running *show slave status* command. In the screen-shot below, both the Slave I/O and SQL threads are running without any error.

```
mysql> show slave status\G
*************************** 1. row ***************************
               Slave_IO_State: Waiting for master to send event
                  Master_Host: mobilestatisticsprofessor.com
                  Master_User: repl
                  Master_Port: 3306
                Connect_Retry: 60
              Master_Log_File: mysql-bin.000005
          Read_Master_Log_Pos: 308
               Relay_Log_File: mysqld-relay-bin.000002
                Relay_Log_Pos: 243
        Relay_Master_Log_File: mysql-bin.000005
             Slave_IO_Running: Yes
            Slave_SQL_Running: Yes
              Replicate_Do_DB:
          Replicate_Ignore_DB:
           Replicate_Do_Table:
       Replicate_Ignore_Table:
      Replicate_Wild_Do_Table:
  Replicate_Wild_Ignore_Table:
                   Last_Errno: 0
                   Last_Error:
                 Skip_Counter: 0
          Exec_Master_Log_Pos: 308
              Relay_Log_Space: 399
              Until_Condition: None
               Until_Log_File:
                Until_Log_Pos: 0
           Master_SSL_Allowed: No
           Master_SSL_CA_File:
           Master_SSL_CA_Path:
              Master_SSL_Cert:
            Master_SSL_Cipher:
               Master_SSL_Key:
        Seconds_Behind_Master: 0
Master_SSL_Verify_Server_Cert: No
                Last_IO_Errno: 0
                Last_IO_Error:
               Last_SQL_Errno: 0
               Last_SQL_Error:
1 row in set (0.00 sec)
```

**Screen-shot 17—21: Show slave status command executed on master host mobilestatisticsprofessor.us.**

Verify processes running on Node by executing *show processlist* command on Node 2.

```
mysql> show processlist\G
*************************** 1. row ***************************
     Id: 5127
   User: repl
   Host: ool-43524ec6.dyn.optonline.net:49588
     db: NULL
Command: Binlog Dump
   Time: 2726
  State: Has sent all binlog to slave; waiting for binlog to be updated
   Info: NULL
*************************** 2. row ***************************
     Id: 5131
   User: root
   Host: localhost
     db: NULL
Command: Query
   Time: 0
  State: NULL
   Info: show processlist
*************************** 3. row ***************************
     Id: 5132
   User: system user
   Host:
     db: NULL
Command: Connect
   Time: 629
  State: Waiting for master to send event
   Info: NULL
*************************** 4. row ***************************
     Id: 5133
   User: system user
   Host:
     db: NULL
Command: Connect
   Time: 628
  State: Has read all relay log; waiting for the slave I/O thread to update it
   Info: NULL
*************************** 5. row ***************************
     Id: 5135
   User: repl
   Host: ip-72-167-246-49.ip.secureserver.net:48906
     db: NULL
Command: Binlog Dump
   Time: 54
  State: Has sent all binlog to slave; waiting for binlog to be updated
   Info: NULL
5 rows in set (0.00 sec)
```

**Screen-shot 17—22: Show processlist command is executed on master mobilestatisticsprofessor.us**

Execute change master command on Node 3 to replicate from master Node 1 and start the slave.

```
mysql> change master to master_host='mobilestatisticsprofessor.com', master_user
='repl', master_password='velcro20', master_log_file='mysql-bin.000005', master_
log_pos=308;
Query OK, 0 rows affected (0.26 sec)

mysql> start slave;
Query OK, 0 rows affected (0.01 sec)
```

Screen-shot 17—23: Change master command executed on ool-43524ec6.dyn.optonline.net:53206. ool-43524ec6.dyn.optonline.net:53206 becomes a slave of master mobilestatisticsproessor.com

Verify slave status on Node 3 by running *show slave status* command. In the screen-shot below, both the Slave I/O and SQL threads are running without any error.

```
mysql> show slave status\G
*********************** 1. row ***********************
               Slave_IO_State: Waiting for master to send event
                  Master_Host: mobilestatisticsprofessor.com
                  Master_User: repl
                  Master_Port: 3306
                Connect_Retry: 60
              Master_Log_File: mysql-bin.000005
          Read_Master_Log_Pos: 308
               Relay_Log_File: mysql-relay-bin.000002
                Relay_Log_Pos: 244
        Relay_Master_Log_File: mysql-bin.000005
             Slave_IO_Running: Yes
            Slave_SQL_Running: Yes
              Replicate_Do_DB:
          Replicate_Ignore_DB:
           Replicate_Do_Table:
       Replicate_Ignore_Table:
      Replicate_Wild_Do_Table:
  Replicate_Wild_Ignore_Table:
                   Last_Errno: 0
                   Last_Error:
                 Skip_Counter: 0
          Exec_Master_Log_Pos: 308
              Relay_Log_Space: 400
              Until_Condition: None
               Until_Log_File:
                Until_Log_Pos: 0
           Master_SSL_Allowed: No
           Master_SSL_CA_File:
           Master_SSL_CA_Path:
              Master_SSL_Cert:
            Master_SSL_Cipher:
               Master_SSL_Key:
        Seconds_Behind_Master: 0
Master_SSL_Verify_Server_Cert: No
                Last_IO_Errno: 0
                Last_IO_Error:
               Last_SQL_Errno: 0
               Last_SQL_Error:
    Replicate_Ignore_Server_Ids:
             Master_Server_Id: 2
1 row in set (0.02 sec)
```

Screen-shot 17—24: Show slave status command is executed on ool-43524ec6.dyn.optonline.net:53206

Verify processes running on Node by executing *show processlist* command on Node 3.

```
*************************** 1. row ***************************
     Id: 352
   User: repl
   Host: 192.254.205.8:56137
     db: NULL
Command: Binlog Dump
   Time: 850
  State: Has sent all binlog to slave; waiting for binlog to be updated
   Info: NULL
*************************** 2. row ***************************
     Id: 366
   User: root
   Host: localhost
     db: NULL
Command: Query
   Time: 0
  State: NULL
   Info: show processlist
*************************** 3. row ***************************
     Id: 370
   User: system user
   Host:
     db: NULL
Command: Connect
   Time: 277
  State: Waiting for master to send event
   Info: NULL
*************************** 4. row ***************************
     Id: 371
   User: system user
   Host:
     db: NULL
Command: Connect
   Time: 276
  State: Has read all relay log; waiting for the slave I/O thread to update it
   Info: NULL
*************************** 5. row ***************************
     Id: 372
   User: repl
   Host: ool-43524ec6.dyn.optonline.net:53206
     db: NULL
Command: Binlog Dump
   Time: 42
  State: Has sent all binlog to slave; waiting for binlog to be updated
   Info: NULL
5 rows in set (0.00 sec)
```

Screen-shot 17—25: Show processlist command is executed on master mobilestatisticsprofessor.com after mobilestatisticsprofessor.us and Ool-43524ec6.dyn.optonline.net:53206 are set up as slaves.

Execute change master command on Node 4 to replicate from master Node 2 and start the slave.

```
mysql> change master to master_host='mobilestatisticsprofessor.us', master_user=
'repl', master_password='velcro20', master_log_file='mysql-bin.000007', master_l
og_pos=2363;
Query OK, 0 rows affected (0.11 sec)

mysql> start slave;
Query OK, 0 rows affected (0.00 sec)
```

**Screen-shot 17—26: Change master command is executed on ool-43524ec6.dyn.optonline.net: 51224. ool-43524ec6.dyn.optonline.net: 51224 becomes a slave of mobilestatisticsprofessor.us.**

Verify slave status on Node 4 by running *show slave status* command. In the screen-shot below, both the Slave I/O and SQL threads are running without any error.

```
mysql> show slave status\G
*************************** 1. row ***************************
               Slave_IO_State: Waiting for master to send event
                  Master_Host: mobilestatisticsprofessor.us
                  Master_User: repl
                  Master_Port: 3306
                Connect_Retry: 60
              Master_Log_File: mysql-bin.000007
          Read_Master_Log_Pos: 2363
               Relay_Log_File: mysql-relay-bin.000002
                Relay_Log_Pos: 252
        Relay_Master_Log_File: mysql-bin.000007
             Slave_IO_Running: Yes
            Slave_SQL_Running: Yes
              Replicate_Do_DB:
          Replicate_Ignore_DB:
           Replicate_Do_Table:
       Replicate_Ignore_Table:
      Replicate_Wild_Do_Table:
  Replicate_Wild_Ignore_Table:
                   Last_Errno: 0
                   Last_Error:
                 Skip_Counter: 0
          Exec_Master_Log_Pos: 2363
              Relay_Log_Space: 408
              Until_Condition: None
               Until_Log_File:
                Until_Log_Pos: 0
           Master_SSL_Allowed: No
           Master_SSL_CA_File:
           Master_SSL_CA_Path:
              Master_SSL_Cert:
            Master_SSL_Cipher:
               Master_SSL_Key:
        Seconds_Behind_Master: 0
Master_SSL_Verify_Server_Cert: No
                Last_IO_Errno: 0
                Last_IO_Error:
               Last_SQL_Errno: 0
               Last_SQL_Error:
   Replicate_Ignore_Server_Ids:
              Master_Server_Id: 1
1 row in set (0.00 sec)
```

Screen-shot 17—27: Show slave status command is executed on slave ool-43524ec6.dyn.optonline.net: 51224.

Verify processes running on Node by executing *show processlist* command on Node 4.

```
mysql> show processlist\G
*************************** 1. row ***************************
     Id: 9
   User: root
   Host: localhost:49727
     db: xignite
Command: Sleep
   Time: 272
  State:
   Info: NULL
*************************** 2. row ***************************
     Id: 10
   User: root
   Host: localhost:49728
     db: xignite
Command: Sleep
   Time: 272
  State:
   Info: NULL
*************************** 3. row ***************************
     Id: 11
   User: root
   Host: piyush-HP:49353
     db: NULL
Command: Query
   Time: 0
  State: NULL
   Info: show processlist
*************************** 4. row ***************************
     Id: 20
   User: repl
   Host: MAC-MINI:49596
     db: NULL
Command: Binlog Dump
   Time: 10091
  State: Master has sent all binlog to slave; waiting for binlog to be updated
   Info: NULL
*************************** 5. row ***************************
     Id: 23
   User: system user
   Host:
     db: NULL
Command: Connect
   Time: 33
  State: Waiting for master to send event
   Info: NULL
*************************** 6. row ***************************
     Id: 24
   User: system user
   Host:
     db: NULL
Command: Connect
   Time: 32
  State: Slave has read all relay log; waiting for the slave I/O thread to updat
e it
   Info: NULL
6 rows in set (0.00 sec)
```

Screen-shot 17—28: Show processlist command is executed on Ool-43524ec6.dyn.optonline.net: 51224.

```
*************************** 2. row ***************************
      Id: 5131
    User: root
    Host: localhost
      db: NULL
 Command: Query
    Time: 0
   State: NULL
    Info: show processlist
*************************** 3. row ***************************
      Id: 5132
    User: system user
    Host:
      db: NULL
 Command: Connect
    Time: 1030
   State: Waiting for master to send event
    Info: NULL
*************************** 4. row ***************************
      Id: 5133
    User: system user
    Host:
      db: NULL
 Command: Connect
    Time: 1029
   State: Has read all relay log; waiting for the slave I/O thread to update it
    Info: NULL
*************************** 5. row ***************************
      Id: 5135
    User: repl
    Host: ip-72-167-246-49.ip.secureserver.net:48906
      db: NULL
 Command: Binlog Dump
    Time: 455
   State: Has sent all binlog to slave; waiting for binlog to be updated
    Info: NULL
*************************** 6. row ***************************
      Id: 5138
    User: repl
    Host: ool-43524ec6.dyn.optonline.net:51224
      db: NULL
 Command: Binlog Dump
    Time: 45
   State: Has sent all binlog to slave; waiting for binlog to be updated
    Info: NULL
6 rows in set (0.00 sec)
```

Screen-shot 17—29: Show processlist command executed on master mobilestatisticsprofessor.us after mobilestatisticsprofessor.com and Ool-43524ec6.dyn.optonline.net: 51224 are set up as slaves.

## 17.6 Summary

This chapter demonstrated how to establish master-master-slave-slave replication.

# 18 Skipping SQL Error

MySQL replication can fail due to SQL error. SQL error could arise from attempt to insert a duplicate key to a slave or attempting to insert into a missing database object. MySQL offers a way to bypass identified SQL errors when specified in the slave's configuration file. The slave needs to be restarted after adding parameter to skip SQL errors. This chapter presents a way to break working master-slave replication. Then, parameter is added to my.cnf and server is restarted. The same experiment is repeated and found that the SQL errors have been bypassed.

## 18.1 Architecture

Physical architecture diagram of master-slave replication configuration is presented below.

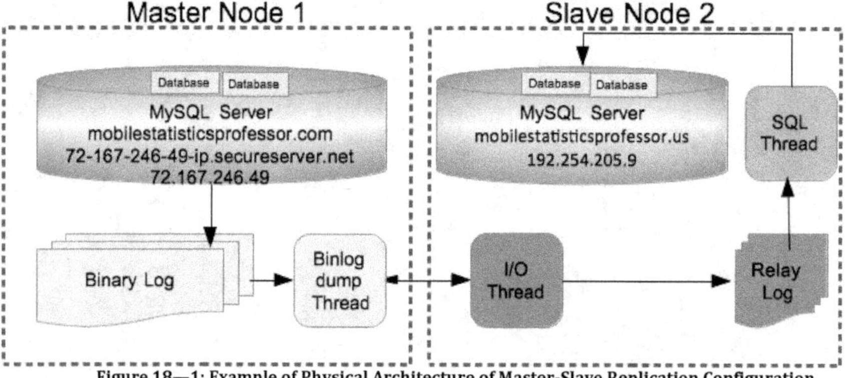


Figure 18—1: Example of Physical Architecture of Master-Slave Replication Configuration

MySQL server host details are presented in the table below.

| Srl. No. | Node | Host/IP Address | server_id | Role |
|---|---|---|---|---|
| 1 | Node 1 | Mobilestatisticsprofessor.com<br>72-167-246-49-ip.secureserver.net<br>72.167.246.49 | 2 | • Node 1 is master of Node 2 |
| 2 | Node 2 | mobilestatisticsprofessor.us,<br>192.254.205.9 | 1 | • Node 2 is slave of Node 1 |

Table 18—1: Master-Master-Active-Passive MySQL Server Configuration

## 18.2 Steps to break and fix replication due to SQL Error

First, a series of commands is executed to break a working master-slave replication. Next, steps are presented to remedy the SQL error and keep the master-slave replication to continue.

### 18.2.1 Break replication

The steps to break replication are as follows.

1.  Create a table in master
2.  Insert data into master
3.  Build unique index in slave
4.  Insert duplicate data to master

### 18.2.2 Fix Replication

The steps to fix broken replication are as follows.

1.  Update slave configuration file to ignore SQL error
2.  Restart slave server
3.  Change master
4.  Start slave
5.  Insert duplicate data to master
6.  Verify status of slave

## 18.3 Detailed Steps

Create a table in the master and insert 3 rows.

```
mysql> create table test_break_repl (id int);
Query OK, 0 rows affected (1.75 sec)

mysql> insert into test_breal_repl values (1);
ERROR 1146 (42S02): Table 'test.test_breal_repl' doesn't exist
mysql> insert into test_break_repl values (1);
Query OK, 1 row affected (0.00 sec)

mysql> insert into test_break_repl values (2);
Query OK, 1 row affected (0.00 sec)

mysql> insert into test_break_repl values (3);
Query OK, 1 row affected (0.00 sec)

mysql> commit;
Query OK, 0 rows affected (0.00 sec)

mysql> select * from test_break_repl;
+--------+
| id     |
+--------+
|      1 |
|      2 |
|      3 |
+--------+
3 rows in set (0.00 sec)
```

Screen-shot 18—1: A table is created in a master to demonstrate the process to break replication and several records are inserted.

The inserted records from master are replicated to the slave as shown below by executing a select on the replicated table in slave.

```
mysql> select * from test_break_repl;
+--------+
| id     |
+--------+
|      1 |
|      2 |
|      3 |
+--------+
3 rows in set (0.00 sec)
```

Screen-shot 18—2: Select query executed on the slave.

A unique index is created on the slave table.

```
mysql> create unique index test_break_repl_idx on test_break_repl (id);
Query OK, 3 rows affected (0.00 sec)
Records: 3  Duplicates: 0  Warnings: 0
```

Screen-shot 18—3: Unique index created on the slave.

Check status of the slave. This screenshot below indicates that both Slave I/O and SQL Threads are running.

```
mysql> show slave status\G
*************************** 1. row ***************************
               Slave_IO_State: Waiting for master to send event
                  Master_Host: mobilestatisticsprofessor.com
                  Master_User: repl
                  Master_Port: 3306
                Connect_Retry: 60
              Master_Log_File: mysql-bin.000003
          Read_Master_Log_Pos: 4963
               Relay_Log_File: mysqld-relay-bin.000002
                Relay_Log_Pos: 646
        Relay_Master_Log_File: mysql-bin.000003
             Slave_IO_Running: Yes
            Slave_SQL_Running: Yes
              Replicate_Do_DB:
          Replicate_Ignore_DB:
           Replicate_Do_Table:
       Replicate_Ignore_Table:
      Replicate_Wild_Do_Table:
  Replicate_Wild_Ignore_Table:
                   Last_Errno: 0
                   Last_Error:
                 Skip_Counter: 0
          Exec_Master_Log_Pos: 4963
              Relay_Log_Space: 802
              Until_Condition: None
               Until_Log_File:
                Until_Log_Pos: 0
           Master_SSL_Allowed: No
           Master_SSL_CA_File:
           Master_SSL_CA_Path:
              Master_SSL_Cert:
            Master_SSL_Cipher:
               Master_SSL_Key:
        Seconds_Behind_Master: 0
Master_SSL_Verify_Server_Cert: No
                Last_IO_Errno: 0
                Last_IO_Error:
               Last_SQL_Errno: 0
               Last_SQL_Error:
1 row in set (0.00 sec)
```

**Screen-shot 18—4: Slave started and slave status is verified**

On master insert a duplicate key value. Master table does not have any unique index. The commit becomes successful on master, but will break replication to slave.

```
mysql> insert into test_break_repl values (3);
Query OK, 1 row affected (0.00 sec)

mysql> commit;
Query OK, 0 rows affected (0.00 sec)

mysql> select * from test_break_repl;
+--------+
| id     |
+--------+
|      1 |
|      2 |
|      3 |
|      3 |
+--------+
4 rows in set (0.00 sec)
```

**Screen-shot 18—5: A new record with duplicate key is inserted into master.**

Check slave status. Notice that the SQL Thread is not running.

```
mysql> show slave status\G
*************************** 1. row ***************************
               Slave_IO_State: Waiting for master to send event
                  Master_Host: mobilestatisticsprofessor.com
                  Master_User: repl
                  Master_Port: 3306
                Connect_Retry: 60
              Master_Log_File: mysql-bin.000003
          Read_Master_Log_Pos: 5064
               Relay_Log_File: mysqld-relay-bin.000002
                Relay_Log_Pos: 646
        Relay_Master_Log_File: mysql-bin.000003
             Slave_IO_Running: Yes
            Slave_SQL_Running: No
              Replicate_Do_DB:
          Replicate_Ignore_DB:
           Replicate_Do_Table:
       Replicate_Ignore_Table:
      Replicate_Wild_Do_Table:
  Replicate_Wild_Ignore_Table:
                   Last_Errno: 1062
                   Last_Error: Error 'Duplicate entry '3' for key 'test_break_re
pl_idx'' on query. Default database: 'test'. Query: 'insert into test_break_repl
 values (3)'
                 Skip_Counter: 0
          Exec_Master_Log_Pos: 4963
              Relay_Log_Space: 903
              Until_Condition: None
               Until_Log_File:
                Until_Log_Pos: 0
           Master_SSL_Allowed: No
           Master_SSL_CA_File:
           Master_SSL_CA_Path:
              Master_SSL_Cert:
            Master_SSL_Cipher:
               Master_SSL_Key:
        Seconds_Behind_Master: NULL
Master_SSL_Verify_Server_Cert: No
                Last_IO_Errno: 0
                Last_IO_Error:
               Last_SQL_Errno: 1062
               Last_SQL_Error: Error 'Duplicate entry '3' for key 'test_break_re
pl_idx'' on query. Default database: 'test'. Query: 'insert into test_break_repl
 values (3)'
1 row in set (0.00 sec)
```

Screen-shot 18—6: Slave status is verified and determination is made that SQL thread is not running


Check the error log on slave. Error related to duplicate key is present.

```
140511  8:35:39 [ERROR] Slave SQL: Error 'Duplicate entry '3' for key 'test_break_repl_idx'' on query
. Default database: 'test'. Query: 'insert into test_break_repl values (3)', Error_code: 1062
140511  8:35:39 [Warning] Slave: Duplicate entry '3' for key 'test_break_repl_idx' Error_code: 1062
140511  8:35:39 [ERROR] Error running query, slave SQL thread aborted. Fix the problem, and restart t
he slave SQL thread with "SLAVE START". We stopped at log 'mysql-bin.000003' position 4963
140511  8:36:31 [Note] Slave I/O thread killed while reading event
```

Screen-shot 18—7: MySQL Error Log is checked for error and the duplicate key error is discovered

Execute show master status on Node 1 and record log file name and position.

```
mysql> show master status;
+------------------+----------+--------------+------------------+
| File             | Position | Binlog_Do_DB | Binlog_Ignore_DB |
+------------------+----------+--------------+------------------+
| mysql-bin.000003 |     5064 |              |                  |
+------------------+----------+--------------+------------------+
1 row in set (0.00 sec)
```

**Screen-shot 18—8: Show master command executed on master to identify binary log coordinates**

On Node 2 (slave), stop replication and reset slave

```
mysql> stop replication;
ERROR 1064 (42000): You have an error in your SQL syntax; check the manual that
corresponds to your MySQL server version for the right syntax to use near 'repli
cation' at line 1
mysql> stop slave;
Query OK, 0 rows affected (0.00 sec)

mysql> reset slave;
Query OK, 0 rows affected (0.00 sec)
```

**Screen-shot 18—9: Slave is stopped and slave is reset.**

On Node 2 (slave), change my.cnf, add slave_skip_errors and bypass error 1062 related to duplicate key insertion.

```
[mysqld]
local-infile=0
max_allowed_packet=16M
set-variable=local-infile=0
datadir=/var/lib/mysql
socket=/var/lib/mysql/mysql.sock
user=mysql
# Default to using old password format for compatibility with mysql 3.x
# clients (those using the mysqlclient10 compatibility package).
old_passwords=1

log_bin=/var/lib/mysql/mysql-bin.log
server_id=1
expire_logs_days=1
slave_skip_error=1062
```

**Screen-shot 18—10: slave_skip_errors is added to MySQL Configuration file my.cnf on the slave**

Restart slave MySQL Server on Node 2.

```
[root@mob ~]# /etc/init.d/mysqld restart
Stopping MySQL:                                            [  OK  ]
Starting MySQL:                                            [  OK  ]
[root@mob ~]#
```

**Screen-shot 18—11: Slave MySQL Server is restarted**

Execute *change master* on Node 2 to replicate from Node 1.

```
mysql> change master to master_host='mobilestatisticsprofessor.com', master_user
='repl', master_password='velcro20', master_log_file='mysql-bin.000003', master_
log_pos=5064;
Query OK, 0 rows affected (0.00 sec)

mysql> start slave;
Query OK, 0 rows affected (0.00 sec)
```

**Screen-shot 18—12: Change master command issued on slave and slave is started**

Check slave status on Node 2. Now, SQL Thread is running.

```
mysql> show slave status\G
*************************** 1. row ***************************
               Slave_IO_State: Waiting for master to send event
                  Master_Host: mobilestatisticsprofessor.com
                  Master_User: repl
                  Master_Port: 3306
                Connect_Retry: 60
              Master_Log_File: mysql-bin.000003
          Read_Master_Log_Pos: 5064
               Relay_Log_File: mysqld-relay-bin.000002
                Relay_Log_Pos: 243
        Relay_Master_Log_File: mysql-bin.000003
             Slave_IO_Running: Yes
            Slave_SQL_Running: Yes
              Replicate_Do_DB:
          Replicate_Ignore_DB:
           Replicate_Do_Table:
       Replicate_Ignore_Table:
      Replicate_Wild_Do_Table:
  Replicate_Wild_Ignore_Table:
                   Last_Errno: 0
                   Last_Error:
                 Skip_Counter: 0
          Exec_Master_Log_Pos: 5064
              Relay_Log_Space: 399
              Until_Condition: None
               Until_Log_File:
                Until_Log_Pos: 0
            Master_SSL_Allowed: No
            Master_SSL_CA_File:
            Master_SSL_CA_Path:
               Master_SSL_Cert:
             Master_SSL_Cipher:
                Master_SSL_Key:
         Seconds_Behind_Master: 0
Master_SSL_Verify_Server_Cert: No
                Last_IO_Errno: 0
                Last_IO_Error:
               Last_SQL_Errno: 0
               Last_SQL_Error:
1 row in set (0.00 sec)
```

**Screen-shot 18—13: Show slave status command executed on slave**

Check the data in the table on Node 1.

```
mysql> select * from test_break_repl;
+-------+
| id    |
+-------+
|     1 |
|     2 |
|     3 |
|     4 |
+-------+
4 rows in set (0.00 sec)
```

**Screen-shot 18—14: Table is queried on master**

Insert a duplicate row to master on Node 1.

```
mysql> insert into test_break_repl values (4);
Query OK, 1 row affected (0.00 sec)

mysql> commit;
Query OK, 0 rows affected (0.00 sec)
```

**Screen-shot 18—15: A new record with duplicate key is inserted into the table in master**

Check slave status on Node 2. SQL Thread is still running.

```
ysql> show slave status\G
*************************** 1. row ***************************
               Slave_IO_State: Waiting for master to send event
                  Master_Host: mobilestatisticsprofessor.com
                  Master_User: repl
                  Master_Port: 3306
                Connect_Retry: 60
              Master_Log_File: mysql-bin.000003
          Read_Master_Log_Pos: 5367
               Relay_Log_File: mysqld-relay-bin.000004
                Relay_Log_Pos: 445
        Relay_Master_Log_File: mysql-bin.000003
             Slave_IO_Running: Yes
            Slave_SQL_Running: Yes
              Replicate_Do_DB:
          Replicate_Ignore_DB:
           Replicate_Do_Table:
       Replicate_Ignore_Table:
      Replicate_Wild_Do_Table:
  Replicate_Wild_Ignore_Table:
                   Last_Errno: 0
                   Last_Error:
                 Skip_Counter: 0
          Exec_Master_Log_Pos: 5367
              Relay_Log_Space: 601
              Until_Condition: None
               Until_Log_File:
                Until_Log_Pos: 0
           Master_SSL_Allowed: No
           Master_SSL_CA_File:
           Master_SSL_CA_Path:
              Master_SSL_Cert:
            Master_SSL_Cipher:
               Master_SSL_Key:
        Seconds_Behind_Master: 0
aster_SSL_Verify_Server_Cert: No
                Last_IO_Errno: 0
                Last_IO_Error:
               Last_SQL_Errno: 0
               Last_SQL_Error:
 row in set (0.00 sec)
```

**Screen-shot 18—16: Show slave status command is executed on slave**

## 18.4  Summary

This chapter demonstrated the process of breaking master-slave replication by inserting duplicate key in un-indexed master table to cause duplicate key error in indexed slave table. Slave_skip_error parameter was added to slave configuration file and slave re-started to bypass the specified SQL errors.

# 19 Using sql_slave_skip_counter to resolve SQL related replication errors

MySQL replication can fail due to SQL error. SQL error could arise from attempt to insert a duplicate key to a slave or attempting to insert into a missing database object. MySQL allows slave to skip a specified number of events from master by setting global variable sql_slave_skip_counter. This chapter explains how to use this through detail example.

## 19.1 Steps to enable sql_slave_skip_counter and resolve the replication issue.

The following 3 commands need to be executed on the slave in order to resolve SQL error events. The number of events $N$ to be skipped needs to be determined by reviewing master's binary log.

1. Stop slave
2. Set global sql_slave_skip_counter = $N$
3. Start slave

## 19.2 How to determine number of events N to skip

To skip one event, use 1 as value of $N$. If the next statement from master uses AUTO_INCREMENT or LAST_INSERT_ID(), then they use two events in binary log; hence, use 2 as the value of $N$.

Value of $N$ can be obtained as follows.

1. Execute show slave status on slave
2. Record the value of Master_Log_File and Exec_Master_Log_Pos
3. View master's binary log file Master_Log_File using mysqlbinlog Unix command and locate the event at Exec_Master_Log_Pos. This will be found after *#at* phrase.
4. Determine the next event from master's binary log file to apply to the slave. Determine the number of events to skip by counting *#at* after step 3 by counting or any other way.

## 19.3 Architecture

Physical architecture diagram of master-slave replication configuration is presented below.

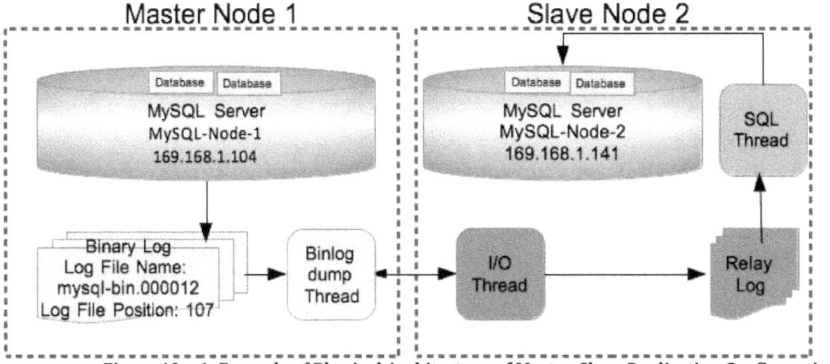


Figure 19—1: Example of Physical Architecture of Master-Slave Replication Configuration

MySQL server host details are presented in the table below.

| Srl. No. | Node | Host/IP Address | server_id | Role |
|---|---|---|---|---|
| 1 | Node 1 | MySQL-Node-1 169.168.1.104 | 11 | • Node 1 is master of Node 2 |
| 2 | Node 2 | MySQL-Node-2 169.168.1.141 | 10 | • Node 2 is slave of Node 1 |

Table 19—1: Master-Slave MySQL Server Configuration

## 19.4 Steps to break and fix replication due to SQL Error

First of master-slave replication is established. A table is created in the master. That table gets replicated to slave. Data is inserted into master table and committed. A unique index is created in slave. Duplicate data is entered into the master table. This breaks replication on slave. Slave is stopped. SQL_Slave_Skip_Counter is set. Then slave is started. Then, slave 's SQL thread starts operating.

### 19.4.1 The steps to break replication are as follows.

The steps to break replication are as follows.

1. Create a table in master
2. Insert data into master
3. Build unique index in slave
4. Insert duplicate data to master

### 19.4.2 Fix Replication

The steps to fix broken replication are as follows.

1. Stop slave
2. Verify status of slave
3. Set global variable SQL_Slave_Skip_Counter to skip a specified number of master events
4. Start slave
5. Insert duplicate data to master

## 19.5 Detailed Steps

Create a table in the master and insert 3 rows.

```
mysql> create table show_skip_counter (col int);
Query OK, 0 rows affected (0.42 sec)

mysql> insert into show_skip_counter values (1), (2), (3);
Query OK, 3 rows affected (0.08 sec)
Records: 3  Duplicates: 0  Warnings: 0

mysql> commit;
Query OK, 0 rows affected (0.00 sec)

mysql> select * from show_skip_counter;
+------+
| col  |
+------+
|    1 |
|    2 |
|    3 |
+------+
3 rows in set (0.01 sec)
```

**Screen-shot 19—1: A table is created in a master to demonstrate the process to break replication and several records are inserted.**

The inserted records from master are replicated to the slave as shown below by executing a select on the replicated table in slave.

```
mysql> use test;
Database changed
mysql> show tables;
+------------------+
| Tables_in_test   |
+------------------+
| show_skip_counter |
| test_auto_inc    |
| test_mysqldump   |
+------------------+
3 rows in set (0.00 sec)

mysql> describe show_skip_counter;
+-------+---------+------+-----+---------+-------+
| Field | Type    | Null | Key | Default | Extra |
+-------+---------+------+-----+---------+-------+
| col   | int(11) | YES  |     | NULL    |       |
+-------+---------+------+-----+---------+-------+
1 row in set (0.07 sec)

mysql> select
    -> * from show_skip_counter;
+------+
| col  |
+------+
|    1 |
|    2 |
|    3 |
+------+
3 rows in set (0.00 sec)
```

Screen-shot 19—2: Select query executed on the slave.

A unique index is created on the slave table.

```
mysql> create unique index show_skip_counter_ux1 on show_skip_counter(col);
Query OK, 0 rows affected (0.10 sec)
Records: 0  Duplicates: 0  Warnings: 0
```

Screen-shot 19—3: Unique index created on the slave.

Check status of the slave. This screenshot below indicates that both Slave I/O and SQL Threads are running.

```
mysql> show slave status\G
*************************** 1. row ***************************
               Slave_IO_State: Waiting for master to send event
                  Master_Host: MySQL-Node-1
                  Master_User: repl
                  Master_Port: 3306
                Connect_Retry: 60
              Master_Log_File: mysql-bin.000012
          Read_Master_Log_Pos: 107
               Relay_Log_File: mysql-relay-bin.000015
                Relay_Log_Pos: 253
        Relay_Master_Log_File: mysql-bin.000012
             Slave_IO_Running: Yes
            Slave_SQL_Running: Yes
              Replicate_Do_DB:
          Replicate_Ignore_DB:
           Replicate_Do_Table:
       Replicate_Ignore_Table:
      Replicate_Wild_Do_Table:
  Replicate_Wild_Ignore_Table:
                   Last_Errno: 0
                   Last_Error:
                 Skip_Counter: 0
          Exec_Master_Log_Pos: 107
              Relay_Log_Space: 409
              Until_Condition: None
               Until_Log_File:
                Until_Log_Pos: 0
           Master_SSL_Allowed: No
           Master_SSL_CA_File:
           Master_SSL_CA_Path:
              Master_SSL_Cert:
            Master_SSL_Cipher:
               Master_SSL_Key:
        Seconds_Behind_Master: 0
Master_SSL_Verify_Server_Cert: No
                Last_IO_Errno: 0
                Last_IO_Error:
               Last_SQL_Errno: 0
               Last_SQL_Error:
  Replicate_Ignore_Server_Ids:
             Master_Server_Id: 11
1 row in set (0.00 sec)
```

**Screen-shot 19—4: Slave started and slave status is verified**

On master insert a duplicate key value. Master table does not have any unique index. The commit becomes successful on master, but will break replication to slave.

```
mysql> insert into show_skip_counter values (4), (5), (6);commit;
Query OK, 3 rows affected (0.24 sec)
Records: 3  Duplicates: 0  Warnings: 0

Query OK, 0 rows affected (0.01 sec)

mysql> insert into show_skip_counter values (6);
Query OK, 1 row affected (0.10 sec)

mysql> commit;
Query OK, 0 rows affected (0.00 sec)
```

**Screen-shot 19—5: A new record with duplicate key is inserted into master.**

Check slave status. Notice that the SQL Thread is not running. Duplicate key error is displayed in Last_SQL_Error column.

```
mysql> show slave status\G
*************************** 1. row ***************************
               Slave_IO_State: Waiting for master to send event
                  Master_Host: MySQL-Node-1
                  Master_User: repl
                  Master_Port: 3306
                Connect_Retry: 60
              Master_Log_File: mysql-bin.000012
          Read_Master_Log_Pos: 859
               Relay_Log_File: mysql-relay-bin.000015
                Relay_Log_Pos: 797
        Relay_Master_Log_File: mysql-bin.000012
             Slave_IO_Running: Yes
            Slave_SQL_Running: No
              Replicate_Do_DB:
          Replicate_Ignore_DB:
           Replicate_Do_Table:
       Replicate_Ignore_Table:
      Replicate_Wild_Do_Table:
  Replicate_Wild_Ignore_Table:
                   Last_Errno: 1062
                   Last_Error: Error 'Duplicate entry '6' for key 'show_skip_cou
nter_ux1'' on query. Default database: 'test'. Query: 'insert into show_skip_cou
nter values (6)'
                 Skip_Counter: 0
          Exec_Master_Log_Pos: 651
              Relay_Log_Space: 1161
              Until_Condition: None
               Until_Log_File:
                Until_Log_Pos: 0
           Master_SSL_Allowed: No
           Master_SSL_CA_File:
           Master_SSL_CA_Path:
              Master_SSL_Cert:
            Master_SSL_Cipher:
               Master_SSL_Key:
        Seconds_Behind_Master: NULL
Master_SSL_Verify_Server_Cert: No
                Last_IO_Errno: 0
                Last_IO_Error:
               Last_SQL_Errno: 1062
               Last_SQL_Error: Error 'Duplicate entry '6' for key 'show_skip_cou
nter_ux1'' on query. Default database: 'test'. Query: 'insert into show_skip_cou
nter values (6)'
   Replicate_Ignore_Server_Ids:
             Master_Server_Id: 11
1 row in set (0.00 sec)
```

Screen-shot 19—6: Slave status is verified and determination is made that SQL thread is not running

On Node 2 (slave), stop slave, set sql_slave_skip_counter to 1 and start the slave.

```
mysql> stop slave;
Query OK, 0 rows affected (0.02 sec)

mysql> set global sql_slave_skip_counter=1;
Query OK, 0 rows affected (0.00 sec)

mysql> start slave;
Query OK, 0 rows affected (0.00 sec)
```

Screen-shot 19—7: Slave is stopped and slave is reset.

Check slave status on Node 2. Now, SQL Thread is running.

```
mysql> show slave status\G
*************************** 1. row ***************************
               Slave_IO_State: Connecting to master
                  Master_Host: MySQL-Node-1
                  Master_User: repl
                  Master_Port: 3306
                Connect_Retry: 60
              Master_Log_File: mysql-bin.000012
          Read_Master_Log_Pos: 859
               Relay_Log_File: mysql-relay-bin.000015
                Relay_Log_Pos: 1005
        Relay_Master_Log_File: mysql-bin.000012
             Slave_IO_Running: Connecting
            Slave_SQL_Running: Yes
              Replicate_Do_DB:
          Replicate_Ignore_DB:
           Replicate_Do_Table:
       Replicate_Ignore_Table:
      Replicate_Wild_Do_Table:
  Replicate_Wild_Ignore_Table:
                   Last_Errno: 0
                   Last_Error:
                 Skip_Counter: 0
          Exec_Master_Log_Pos: 859
              Relay_Log_Space: 1161
              Until_Condition: None
               Until_Log_File:
                Until_Log_Pos: 0
           Master_SSL_Allowed: No
           Master_SSL_CA_File:
           Master_SSL_CA_Path:
              Master_SSL_Cert:
            Master_SSL_Cipher:
               Master_SSL_Key:
        Seconds_Behind_Master: NULL
Master_SSL_Verify_Server_Cert: No
                Last_IO_Errno: 0
                Last_IO_Error:
               Last_SQL_Errno: 0
               Last_SQL_Error:
  Replicate_Ignore_Server_Ids:
             Master_Server_Id: 11
1 row in set (0.00 sec)
```

**Screen-shot 19—8: Show slave status command executed on slave**

## 19.6 Summary

This chapter demonstrated the process of breaking master-slave replication by inserting duplicate key in un-indexed master table to cause duplicate key error in indexed slave table. It explains how to determine the number of events to skip. SQL_Slave_Skip_Counter parameter was set to skip specified number of master events to allow slave SQL process to start working again.

# 20 Experimenting with auto increment to break replication

Tables can be created to generate value for key columns using auto_increment. Auto_increment generates key value using auto_increment_offset and auto_increment_increment session variables. By default, auto_increment_offset is set to 1 and auto_increment_increment set to 1. If these values are left unchanged, then the auto_increment values generated is 1, 2, 3, and 4.... This type of value for key columns can raise duplicate key error in case master and slave attempt to insert into a table simultaneously. MySQL offers a fix for such scenario. These variables can be set up using MySQL session or configuration file to generate unique auto_increment value in a replication configuration involving multiple servers.

First, this chapter explores steps to break and next to fix replication-setting values to generate unique auto_increment value.

## 20.1 Steps to break replication through collision of key value

The steps to break replication are as follows.

1. Establish bi-directional replication between two masters
2. Create a table with auto_increment column as primary key.
3. Insert several records to the table in each master simultaneously
4. Keep checking the slave status on each until the slave SQL threads stop running on either
5. If needed insert more records until SQL thread stops running on either of the masters

Two global variables, auto_increment_increment and auto_increment_offset control the generated value for the auto_increment column. By default, these are set to 1. The generated value starts with the value of the auto_increment_offset. Then, the value gets incremented by auto_increment_increment on each subsequent generation of auto_increment value.

Default values generated for auto_increment column are 1, 2, and 3,-.$2^{32}$-1.

Let's change the auto_increment_increment is set to 3 and auto_increment_offset is set to 1.

Now, the generated auto_increment values are 1, 4, 7, 10....$2^{32}$-1.

Let's change the auto_increment_increment is set to 3 and auto_increment_offset is set to 2.

Now, the generated auto_increment values are 2, 5, 8, 11....$2^{32}$-1.

The generated auto_increment value is auto_increment_offset + auto_increment_increment x N where N is the Nth time the value is beginning generated.

## 20.2 Remedy

To remedy the key value collision for keys using auto_increment, set auto_increment_increment and auto_increment_offset in each master participating in replication. In case user updates are allowed in a slave, these variables can be set up as well.

Best practice to set up the value of these variables is as follows.

**auto_increment_increment = N + 1 where N is the number of servers in replication topology**

**auto_increment_offset = an integer between 1 and N**

## 20.3 Example

First, the working replication is broken and next remedy is presented to fix the broken replication.

### 20.3.1 Breaking replication

Two servers, mobilestatisticsprofessor.com and mobilestatisticsprofessor.us servers established bi-directional replication.

Value of the auto_increment variables in mobilestaisticsprofessor.com is as follows.

```
mysql> show variables like 'auto_inc%';
+-------------------------------+-------+
| Variable_name                 | Value |
+-------------------------------+-------+
| auto_increment_increment      | 1     |
| auto_increment_offset         | 1     |
+-------------------------------+-------+
2 rows in set (0.00 sec)
```

**Screen-shot 20—1: Query auto_increment_increment and auto_increment_offset variables on master host mobilestatisticsprofessor.com**

Value of the auto_increment variables in mobilestaisticsprofessor.us is as follows.

```
mysql> show variables like 'auto_inc%';
+-------------------------+-------+
| Variable_name           | Value |
+-------------------------+-------+
| auto_increment_increment | 1    |
| auto_increment_offset   | 1     |
+-------------------------+-------+
2 rows in set (0.00 sec)
```

**Screen-shot 20—2: Query auto_increment_increment and auto_increment_offset variables on master mobilestatisticsprofessor.us**

Create a table with an auto_increment column in mobilestaisticsprofessor.com.

```
mysql> use test;
Reading table information for completion of table and column names
You can turn off this feature to get a quicker startup with -A

Database changed
mysql> create table test_auto_inc (id int not null auto_increment primary key);
Query OK, 0 rows affected (0.04 sec)
```

**Screen-shot 20—3: Create table in mobilestatisticsprofesor.com with an auto_increment column**

Create a table with an auto_increment column in mobilestaisticsprofessor.us.

```
mysql> create table test_auto_inc (id int not null auto_increment primary key);
Query OK, 0 rows affected (0.00 sec)
```

**Screen-shot 20—4: Create a table in mobilestatisticsprofessor.us with an auto_increment column**

Record log coordinates of mobilestaisticsprofessor.us.

```
mysql> show master status\G
*************************** 1. row ***************************
            File: mysql-bin.000010
        Position: 240
    Binlog_Do_DB:
Binlog_Ignore_DB:
1 row in set (0.00 sec)
```

**Screen-shot 20—5: Query master status on mobilestatisticsprofessor.us**

Execute *change master* to command on mobilestaisticsprofessor.com to replicate from mobilestatisticsprofessor.us.

```
mysql> change master to master_host='mobilestatisticsprofessor.us', master_user=
'repl', master_password='velcro20', master_log_file='mysql-bin.000010', master_l
og_pos=240;
Query OK, 0 rows affected (0.75 sec)

mysql> start slave;
Query OK, 0 rows affected (0.00 sec)
```

**Screen-shot 20—6: Query master status and establish replication with mobilestatisticsprofessor.us from mobilestatisticsprofessor.com**

## Check slave status on mobilestatisticsprofessor.com.

```
mysql> show slave status\G
*************************** 1. row ***************************
               Slave_IO_State: Waiting for master to send event
                  Master_Host: mobilestatisticsprofessor.us
                  Master_User: repl
                  Master_Port: 3306
                Connect_Retry: 60
              Master_Log_File: mysql-bin.000010
          Read_Master_Log_Pos: 240
               Relay_Log_File: mysqld-relay-bin.000002
                Relay_Log_Pos: 243
        Relay_Master_Log_File: mysql-bin.000010
             Slave_IO_Running: Yes
            Slave_SQL_Running: Yes
              Replicate_Do_DB:
          Replicate_Ignore_DB:
           Replicate_Do_Table:
       Replicate_Ignore_Table:
      Replicate_Wild_Do_Table:
  Replicate_Wild_Ignore_Table:
                   Last_Errno: 0
                   Last_Error:
                 Skip_Counter: 0
          Exec_Master_Log_Pos: 240
              Relay_Log_Space: 243
              Until_Condition: None
               Until_Log_File:
                Until_Log_Pos: 0
           Master_SSL_Allowed: No
           Master_SSL_CA_File:
           Master_SSL_CA_Path:
              Master_SSL_Cert:
            Master_SSL_Cipher:
               Master_SSL_Key:
        Seconds_Behind_Master: 0
1 row in set (0.00 sec)
```

**Screen-shot 20—7: Show slave status on mobilestatisticsprofessor.com**

Record log coordinates of mobilestaisticsprofessor.com.

```
mysql> show master status\G
*************************** 1. row ***************************
            File: mysql-bin.000007
        Position: 232
    Binlog_Do_DB:
Binlog_Ignore_DB:
1 row in set (0.00 sec)
```

**Screen-shot 20—8: Query master status on mobilestatisticsprofessor.com**

Execute *change master* to command on mobilestaisticsprofessor.com to replicate from mobilestatisticsprofessor.us.

```
mysql> change master to master_host='mobilestatisticsprofessor.com', master_user
='repl', master_password='velcro20', master_log_file='mysql-bin.000007', master_
log_pos=232;
Query OK, 0 rows affected (0.00 sec)

mysql> start slave;
Query OK, 0 rows affected (0.00 sec)
```

**Screen-shot 20—9: Issue change master command on mobilestatisticsprofessor.us**

Check slave status on mobilestatisticsprofessor.us.

```
mysql> show slave status\G
*************************** 1. row ***************************
               Slave_IO_State: Waiting for master to send event
                  Master_Host: mobilestatisticsprofessor.com
                  Master_User: repl
                  Master_Port: 3306
                Connect_Retry: 60
              Master_Log_File: mysql-bin.000007
          Read_Master_Log_Pos: 232
               Relay_Log_File: mysqld-relay-bin.000002
                Relay_Log_Pos: 243
        Relay_Master_Log_File: mysql-bin.000007
             Slave_IO_Running: Yes
            Slave_SQL_Running: Yes
              Replicate_Do_DB:
          Replicate_Ignore_DB:
           Replicate_Do_Table:
       Replicate_Ignore_Table:
      Replicate_Wild_Do_Table:
  Replicate_Wild_Ignore_Table:
                   Last_Errno: 0
                   Last_Error:
                 Skip_Counter: 0
          Exec_Master_Log_Pos: 232
              Relay_Log_Space: 399
              Until_Condition: None
               Until_Log_File:
                Until_Log_Pos: 0
           Master_SSL_Allowed: No
           Master_SSL_CA_File:
           Master_SSL_CA_Path:
              Master_SSL_Cert:
            Master_SSL_Cipher:
               Master_SSL_Key:
        Seconds_Behind_Master: 0
Master_SSL_Verify_Server_Cert: No
                Last_IO_Errno: 0
```

Screen-shot 20—10: Show status of slave on mobilestatisticsprofessor.us

Insert several records to the table in mobilestatistcsprofessor.com.

```
mysql> select * from test_auto_inc;
+-----+
| id |
+-----+
|   1 |
|   2 |
|   3 |
|   4 |
|   5 |
|   6 |
|   7 |
|   8 |
|   9 |
|  10 |
+-----+
10 rows in set (0.00 sec)

mysql> insert into test_auto_inc values (null),(null),(null);commit;
Query OK, 3 rows affected (0.00 sec)
Records: 3  Duplicates: 0  Warnings: 0

Query OK, 0 rows affected (0.00 sec)
```

**Screen-shot 20—11: Query table with auto_increment table and insert few records in mobilestatisticsprofessor.com**

Insert several records to the table in mobilestatistcsprofessor.us.

```
mysql>  insert into test_auto_inc values (null),(null),(null);
Query OK, 3 rows affected (0.00 sec)
Records: 3  Duplicates: 0  Warnings: 0

mysql> commit;
Query OK, 0 rows affected (0.00 sec)

mysql> select * from test_auto_inc;
+-----+
| id |
+-----+
|   1 |
|   2 |
|   3 |
|   4 |
|   5 |
|   6 |
|   7 |
|   8 |
|   9 |
|  10 |
+-----+
10 rows in set (0.00 sec)
```

**Screen-shot 20—12: Insert several records to the auto_increment table and select the table in mobilestatisticsprofessor.us**

Insert several more records to the table in mobilestatistcsprofessor.us.

```
mysql> insert into test_auto_inc values (null),(null),(null),(null);
Query OK, 4 rows affected (0.00 sec)
Records: 4  Duplicates: 0  Warnings: 0

mysql> commit;
Query OK, 0 rows affected (0.00 sec)

mysql> select * from test_auto_inc;
+------+
| id |
+------+
|    1 |
|    2 |
|    3 |
|    4 |
|    5 |
|    6 |
|    7 |
|    8 |
|    9 |
|   10 |
|   11 |
|   12 |
|   13 |
|   14 |
+------+
14 rows in set (0.00 sec)
```

**Screen-shot 20—13: Insert into mobilestatisticsprofessor.us auto_increment table**

Check slave status on mobilestatisticsprofessor.com. SQL Thread is not running.

```
mysql> select * from test_auto_inc;
+----+
| id |
+----+
|  1 |
|  2 |
|  3 |
|  4 |
|  5 |
|  6 |
|  7 |
|  8 |
|  9 |
| 10 |
| 11 |
| 12 |
| 13 |
+----+
13 rows in set (0.00 sec)

mysql> show slave status\G
*************************** 1. row ***************************
               Slave_IO_State: Waiting for master to send event
                  Master_Host: mobilestatisticsprofessor.us
                  Master_User: repl
                  Master_Port: 3306
                Connect_Retry: 60
              Master_Log_File: mysql-bin.000010
          Read_Master_Log_Pos: 798
               Relay_Log_File: mysqld-relay-bin.000002
                Relay_Log_Pos: 647
        Relay_Master_Log_File: mysql-bin.000010
             Slave_IO_Running: Yes
            Slave_SQL_Running: No
```

**Screen-shot 20—14: Query on auto_increment table and check slave status on mobilestatisticsprofessor.com. Replication Slave SQL process is not running.**

Check error log in mobilestatisticsprofessor.com. Duplicate key error is located.

```
140515 17:56:49 [ERROR] Slave: Error 'Duplicate entry '11' for key 1' on query.
Default database: 'test'. Query: 'insert into test_auto_inc values (null), (null
), (null), (null)', Error_code: 1062
140515 17:56:49 [ERROR] Error running query, slave SQL thread aborted. Fix the p
roblem, and restart the slave SQL thread with "SLAVE START". We stopped at log '
mysql-bin.000010' position 644
[root@ip-72-167-246-49 ~]#
```

**Screen-shot 20—15: Check MySQL Error Log on mobilestatisticsprofessor.com and locate the SQL error that broke replication.**

### 20.3.2 Fixing Replication

To remedy the issue, set up auto_increment_increment and auto_increment_offset values in my.cnf files of each server to generate unique auto_increment values. Restart the server after changes are made.

In mobilestatisticsprofessor.com, add the following to my.cnf file.

*auto_increment_offset=1*
*auto_increment_increment=3*
In mobilestatisticsprofessor.com, add the following to my.cnf file.

*auto_increment_offset=2*
*auto_increment_increment=3*

Restart MySQL server on both the hosts.


## 20.4 Summary

This chapter discussed auto_increment variables, how to break replication by keeping the default values and how to remedy broken replication due to auto_increment value collision.

# 21 Interpreting output of Show slave status

MySQL offers *show status* command to check the status of a slave. This chapter describes how to interpret the output and spot common SQL as well as I/O errors.

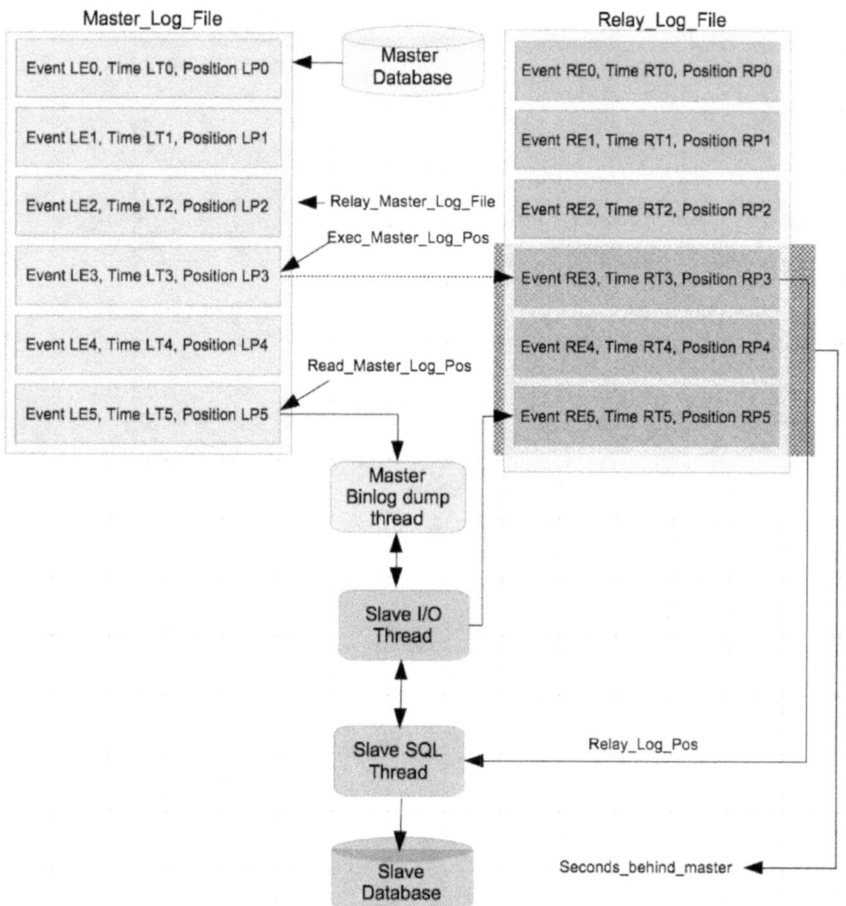


Figure 21—1: Key show slave status parameters presented visually

Figure 20-1 depicts key slaves, files, events and show slave status variables. In this figure, LE represents log event. LT represents log time and LP represents log position. RE represents relay log event, RT represents relay log rime and RP represents relay log position. Master Binlog dump thread is initiated when slave is started. Master Binlog dump thread reads master's binary log and sends the log events to slave's I/O Thread. Slave starts

I/O and SQL thread when slave is started. Slave I/O writes to master binary log events to relay log file. Slave SQL thread reads relay log events and replays them on slave database.

The important variables are presented below along with examples and interpretation.

| Variable | Interpretation | Example from healthy state |
| --- | --- | --- |
| Slave_IO_State | State of I/O Thread | Waiting for master to send event |
| Master_Host | Master host name | mobilestatisticsprofessor.com |
| Master_User | User account on master that slave is using to replicate | repl |
| Master_Port | Master port slave is using to connect | 3306 |
| Connect_Retry | How many times slave will try before stopping connection attempts | 60 |
| Master_Log_File | Master log file master's Binlog dump process is reading | mysql-bin.000008 |
| Read_Master_Log_Pos | Master log file position master's Binlog dump thread has read | 98 |
| Relay_Log_File | Name of relay log file on slave that slave's SQL thread is reading and replaying | mysqld-relay-bin.000002 |
| Relay_Log_Pos | Position in relay log file up to which slave's SQL thread has read and executed up to | 243 |
| Relay_Master_Log_File | Which master log file corresponds to the event executed by slave's SQL thread? | mysql-bin.000008 |
| Slave_IO_Running | Is slave I/O thread running? | Yes |
| Slave_SQL_Running | Is slave SQL thread running? | Yes |
| Last_Errno | What is last error number? Value 0 is healthy. Anything, but 0 is problem state. | 0 |
| Last_Error | Blank is healthy. Non-blank is problem state. | |
| Exec_Master_Log_Pos | The master binary log position the slave SQL thread has read (via relay log) and executed | 98 |

| Variable | Interpretation | Example from healthy state |
|---|---|---|
|  |  |  |
| Seconds_Behind_ Master | Lag between the slave I/O and SQL thread. Non-zero seconds indicates how far the slave is behind. | 0 |
| Last_IO_Errno | I/O error number. Healthy state is 0. Problem state is non-zero. | 0 |
| Last_IO_Error | Healthy state is blank. Error description will appear in case of error. |  |
| Last_SQL_Errno | SQL error number. Healthy state is 0. Problem state is non-zero. | 0 |
| Last_SQL_Error | Healthy state is blank. Error description will appear in case of error. |  |

Table 21—1: Key variables displayed when show slave status command is executed on slave

## 21.1 When slave is not running

Slave_IO_State is blank or null when slave is not running. Slave_IO_running is No and Slave_SQL_Running is No. In this state, the error numbers will contain 0 and error description will be blank.

```
mysql> show slave status\G
*************************** 1. row ***************************
               Slave_IO_State:
                  Master_Host: mobilestatisticsprofessor.com
                  Master_User: repl
                  Master_Port: 3306
                Connect_Retry: 60
              Master_Log_File: mysql-bin.000008
          Read_Master_Log_Pos: 98
               Relay_Log_File: mysqld-relay-bin.000015
                Relay_Log_Pos: 243
        Relay_Master_Log_File: mysql-bin.000008
             Slave_IO_Running: No
            Slave_SQL_Running: No
              Replicate_Do_DB:
          Replicate_Ignore_DB:
           Replicate_Do_Table:
       Replicate_Ignore_Table:
      Replicate_Wild_Do_Table:
  Replicate_Wild_Ignore_Table:
                   Last_Errno: 0
                   Last_Error:
                 Skip_Counter: 0
          Exec_Master_Log_Pos: 98
              Relay_Log_Space: 536
              Until_Condition: None
               Until_Log_File:
                Until_Log_Pos: 0
           Master_SSL_Allowed: No
           Master_SSL_CA_File:
           Master_SSL_CA_Path:
              Master_SSL_Cert:
            Master_SSL_Cipher:
               Master_SSL_Key:
        Seconds_Behind_Master: NULL
Master_SSL_Verify_Server_Cert: No
                Last_IO_Errno: 0
                Last_IO_Error:
               Last_SQL_Errno: 0
               Last_SQL_Error:
1 row in set (0.02 sec)
```

**Screen-shot 21—1: Show slave status command executed when slave is not running**

## 21.2  When slave is running without any error.

Slave_IO_running is yes and Slave_SQL_Running is Yes.  Last_IO_Error_no is 0 and Last_IO_Error is blank. Last_SQL_Error_no is 0 and Last_SQL_Error is blank. Second_Behind_Master is 0 or small.

```
mysql> show slave status\G
*************************** 1. row ***************************
               Slave_IO_State: Waiting for master to send event
                  Master_Host: mobilestatisticsprofessor.com
                  Master_User: repl
                  Master_Port: 3306
                Connect_Retry: 60
              Master_Log_File: mysql-bin.000008
          Read_Master_Log_Pos: 98
               Relay_Log_File: mysqld-relay-bin.000002
                Relay_Log_Pos: 243
        Relay_Master_Log_File: mysql-bin.000008
             Slave_IO_Running: Yes
            Slave_SQL_Running: Yes
              Replicate_Do_DB:
          Replicate_Ignore_DB:
           Replicate_Do_Table:
       Replicate_Ignore_Table:
      Replicate_Wild_Do_Table:
  Replicate_Wild_Ignore_Table:
                   Last_Errno: 0
                   Last_Error:
                 Skip_Counter: 0
          Exec_Master_Log_Pos: 98
              Relay_Log_Space: 399
              Until_Condition: None
               Until_Log_File:
                Until_Log_Pos: 0
           Master_SSL_Allowed: No
           Master_SSL_CA_File:
           Master_SSL_CA_Path:
              Master_SSL_Cert:
            Master_SSL_Cipher:
               Master_SSL_Key:
        Seconds_Behind_Master: 0
Master_SSL_Verify_Server_Cert: No
                Last_IO_Errno: 0
                Last_IO_Error:
               Last_SQL_Errno: 0
               Last_SQL_Error:
1 row in set (0.00 sec)
```

Screen-shot 21—2: Show slave status command is executed when slave is running successfully

## 21.3  Slave running with I/O errors

Slave_IO_running is No. Last_IO_Error_no is non-zero integer and Last_IO_Error will contain the error message.

### 21.3.1 I/O Error arising due to duplicate server ids

I/O error 1593 manifests when the master and slave use the same server_id.

```
mysql> show slave status\G
*************************** 1. row ***************************
               Slave_IO_State:
                  Master_Host: mobilestatisticsprofessor.com
                  Master_User: repl
                  Master_Port: 3306
                Connect_Retry: 60
              Master_Log_File: mysql-bin.000008
          Read_Master_Log_Pos: 98
               Relay_Log_File: mysqld-relay-bin.000001
                Relay_Log_Pos: 4
        Relay_Master_Log_File: mysql-bin.000008
             Slave_IO_Running: No
            Slave_SQL_Running: Yes
              Replicate_Do_DB:
          Replicate_Ignore_DB:
           Replicate_Do_Table:
       Replicate_Ignore_Table:
      Replicate_Wild_Do_Table:
  Replicate_Wild_Ignore_Table:
                   Last_Errno: 0
                   Last_Error:
                 Skip_Counter: 0
          Exec_Master_Log_Pos: 98
              Relay_Log_Space: 106
              Until_Condition: None
               Until_Log_File:
                Until_Log_Pos: 0
           Master_SSL_Allowed: No
           Master_SSL_CA_File:
           Master_SSL_CA_Path:
              Master_SSL_Cert:
            Master_SSL_Cipher:
               Master_SSL_Key:
        Seconds_Behind_Master: NULL
Master_SSL_Verify_Server_Cert: No
                Last_IO_Errno: 1593
                Last_IO_Error: Fatal error: The slave I/O thread stops because
aster and slave have equal MySQL server ids; these ids must be different for re
lication to work (or the --replicate-same-server-id option must be used on slav
 but this does not always make sense; please check the manual before using it).
               Last_SQL_Errno: 0
               Last_SQL_Error:
1 row in set (0.00 sec)
```
**Screen-shot 21—3: I/O Error 1593 due to duplicate server_id**

## 21.3.2 I/O Errors arising due to Connectivity Issue

As an example when slave replication account is not able to connect to the master. This could occur due to not having replication account in the master, incorrect user id or password or slave host not having permission to connect to the master as well as firewall issues. Error 1045 indicates that there is issue related to the replication user account. Error 1130 indicates that the slave host is not allowed to connect to the master host.

```
mysql> show slave status\G
*************************** 1. row ***************************
               Slave_IO_State: Connecting to master
                  Master_Host: mobilestatisticsprofessor.com
                  Master_User: repl12
                  Master_Port: 3306
                Connect_Retry: 60
              Master_Log_File: mysql-bin.000008
          Read_Master_Log_Pos: 98
               Relay_Log_File: mysqld-relay-bin.000001
                Relay_Log_Pos: 4
        Relay_Master_Log_File: mysql-bin.000008
             Slave_IO_Running: No
            Slave_SQL_Running: Yes
              Replicate_Do_DB:
          Replicate_Ignore_DB:
           Replicate_Do_Table:
       Replicate_Ignore_Table:
      Replicate_Wild_Do_Table:
  Replicate_Wild_Ignore_Table:
                   Last_Errno: 0
                   Last_Error:
                 Skip_Counter: 0
          Exec_Master_Log_Pos: 98
              Relay_Log_Space: 106
              Until_Condition: None
               Until_Log_File:
                Until_Log_Pos: 0
           Master_SSL_Allowed: No
           Master_SSL_CA_File:
           Master_SSL_CA_Path:
              Master_SSL_Cert:
            Master_SSL_Cipher:
               Master_SSL_Key:
        Seconds_Behind_Master: NULL
Master_SSL_Verify_Server_Cert: No
                Last_IO_Errno: 1045
                Last_IO_Error: error connecting to master 'repl12@mobilestatisti
csprofessor.com:3306' - retry-time: 60  retries: 86400
               Last_SQL_Errno: 0
               Last_SQL_Error:
1 row in set (0.00 sec)
```

**Screen-shot 21—4: Show slave status where I/O error 1045 is encountered**

### 21.3.3  I/O Error arising due to log file name and position issues

Log file name, position or checksum can raise error 1236 and stop I/O thread.

As an example, when log file name is not specified correctly error 1236 manifests.

```
mysql> show slave status\G
*************************** 1. row ***************************
               Slave_IO_State:
                  Master_Host: mobilestatisticsprofessor.com
                  Master_User: repl
                  Master_Port: 3306
                Connect_Retry: 60
              Master_Log_File: mysql-bin.0000012
          Read_Master_Log_Pos: 98
               Relay_Log_File: mysqld-relay-bin.000001
                Relay_Log_Pos: 4
        Relay_Master_Log_File: mysql-bin.0000012
             Slave_IO_Running: No
            Slave_SQL_Running: Yes
              Replicate_Do_DB:
          Replicate_Ignore_DB:
           Replicate_Do_Table:
       Replicate_Ignore_Table:
      Replicate_Wild_Do_Table:
  Replicate_Wild_Ignore_Table:
                   Last_Errno: 0
                   Last_Error:
                 Skip_Counter: 0
          Exec_Master_Log_Pos: 98
              Relay_Log_Space: 106
              Until_Condition: None
               Until_Log_File:
                Until_Log_Pos: 0
           Master_SSL_Allowed: No
           Master_SSL_CA_File:
           Master_SSL_CA_Path:
              Master_SSL_Cert:
            Master_SSL_Cipher:
               Master_SSL_Key:
        Seconds_Behind_Master: NULL
Master_SSL_Verify_Server_Cert: No
                Last_IO_Errno: 1236
                Last_IO_Error: Got fatal error 1236 from master when reading dat
a from binary log: 'Could not find first log file name in binary log index file'
               Last_SQL_Errno: 0
               Last_SQL_Error:
1 row in set (0.00 sec)
```

**Screen-shot 21—5: Show slave status displays I/O error 1236**

As **log file position** is not specified correctly, 1236 error is manifested.

```
mysql> show slave status\G
*************************** 1. row ***************************
               Slave_IO_State:
                  Master_Host: mobilestatisticsprofessor.com
                  Master_User: repl
                  Master_Port: 3306
                Connect_Retry: 60
              Master_Log_File: mysql-bin.000008
          Read_Master_Log_Pos: 900
               Relay_Log_File: mysqld-relay-bin.000001
                Relay_Log_Pos: 4
        Relay_Master_Log_File: mysql-bin.000008
             Slave_IO_Running: No
            Slave_SQL_Running: Yes
              Replicate_Do_DB:
          Replicate_Ignore_DB:
           Replicate_Do_Table:
       Replicate_Ignore_Table:
      Replicate_Wild_Do_Table:
  Replicate_Wild_Ignore_Table:
                   Last_Errno: 0
                   Last_Error:
                 Skip_Counter: 0
          Exec_Master_Log_Pos: 900
              Relay_Log_Space: 106
              Until_Condition: None
               Until_Log_File:
                Until_Log_Pos: 0
           Master_SSL_Allowed: No
           Master_SSL_CA_File:
           Master_SSL_CA_Path:
              Master_SSL_Cert:
            Master_SSL_Cipher:
               Master_SSL_Key:
        Seconds_Behind_Master: NULL
Master_SSL_Verify_Server_Cert: No
                Last_IO_Errno: 1236
                Last_IO_Error: Got fatal error 1236 from master when reading dat
a from binary log: 'Client requested master to start replication from impossible
 position'
               Last_SQL_Errno: 0
               Last_SQL_Error:
1 row in set (0.00 sec)
```

Screen-shot 21—6: Show slave status demonstrating another type of 1236 I/O error

## 21.3.4 I/O Error due to checksum mismatch

I/O error 1236 can arise due to **checksum** error. This arises due to different MySQL version on master and slave. To remedy this type of issue, configure master my.cnf to binlog-checksum=none.

```
mysql> show slave status\G
*********************** 1. row ***********************
               Slave_IO_State:
                  Master_Host: Mac-Mini.local
                  Master_User: repl
                  Master_Port: 3306
                Connect_Retry: 60
              Master_Log_File: Mac-Mini-bin.000008
          Read_Master_Log_Pos: 2467
               Relay_Log_File: mysql-relay-bin.000002
                Relay_Log_Pos: 153
        Relay_Master_Log_File: Mac-Mini-bin.000008
             Slave_IO_Running: No
            Slave_SQL_Running: Yes
              Replicate_Do_DB:
          Replicate_Ignore_DB:
           Replicate_Do_Table:
       Replicate_Ignore_Table:
      Replicate_Wild_Do_Table:
  Replicate_Wild_Ignore_Table:
                   Last_Errno: 0
                   Last_Error:
                 Skip_Counter: 0
          Exec_Master_Log_Pos: 2467
              Relay_Log_Space: 309
              Until_Condition: None
               Until_Log_File:
                Until_Log_Pos: 0
           Master_SSL_Allowed: No
           Master_SSL_CA_File:
           Master_SSL_CA_Path:
              Master_SSL_Cert:
            Master_SSL_Cipher:
               Master_SSL_Key:
        Seconds_Behind_Master: NULL
Master_SSL_Verify_Server_Cert: No
                Last_IO_Errno: 1236
                Last_IO_Error: Got fatal error 1236 from master when reading dat
a from binary log: 'Slave can not handle replication events with the checksum th
at master is configured to log; the first event 'Mac-Mini-bin.000008' at 2467, t
he last event read from './Mac-Mini-bin.000008' at 2467, the last byte read from
 './Mac-Mini-bin.000008' at 120.'
               Last_SQL_Errno: 0
               Last_SQL_Error:
  Replicate_Ignore_Server_Ids:
             Master_Server_Id: 1000
1 row in set (0.00 sec)
```

Screen-shot 21—7: I/O error due to checksum error

Versions of Master and Slave are different. Master's version is 5.6.10-log where as the slave's version is 5.5.29-log. Slave's version is higher than that of the master.

```
mysql> select version();
+------------+
| version()  |
+------------+
| 5.6.10-log |
+------------+
1 row in set (0.12 sec)
```

Screen-shot 21—8: Master's MySQL version

```
mysql> select version();
+------------+
| version()  |
+------------+
| 5.5.29-log |
+------------+
1 row in set (0.00 sec)
```

Screen-shot 21—9: Slave's MySQL version

## 21.4 Slave running with SQL Errors

Slave_SQL_running is No. Last_SQL_Error_no is non-zero integer and Last_SQL_Error will contain the error message.

### 21.4.1 SQL Error due to duplicate value

As an example of duplicate key SQL error is presented below.

```
mysql> show slave status\G
*************************** 1. row ***************************
               Slave_IO_State: Waiting for master to send event
                  Master_Host: mobilestatisticsprofessor.com
                  Master_User: repl
                  Master_Port: 3306
                Connect_Retry: 60
              Master_Log_File: mysql-bin.000003
          Read_Master_Log_Pos: 5064
               Relay_Log_File: mysqld-relay-bin.000002
                Relay_Log_Pos: 646
        Relay_Master_Log_File: mysql-bin.000003
             Slave_IO_Running: Yes
            Slave_SQL_Running: No
              Replicate_Do_DB:
          Replicate_Ignore_DB:
           Replicate_Do_Table:
       Replicate_Ignore_Table:
      Replicate_Wild_Do_Table:
  Replicate_Wild_Ignore_Table:
                   Last_Errno: 1062
                   Last_Error: Error 'Duplicate entry '3' for key 'test_break_re
pl_idx'' on query. Default database: 'test'. Query: 'insert into test_break_repl
 values (3)'
                 Skip_Counter: 0
          Exec_Master_Log_Pos: 4963
              Relay_Log_Space: 903
              Until_Condition: None
               Until_Log_File:
                Until_Log_Pos: 0
           Master_SSL_Allowed: No
           Master_SSL_CA_File:
           Master_SSL_CA_Path:
              Master_SSL_Cert:
            Master_SSL_Cipher:
               Master_SSL_Key:
        Seconds_Behind_Master: NULL
Master_SSL_Verify_Server_Cert: No
                Last_IO_Errno: 0
                Last_IO_Error:
               Last_SQL_Errno: 1062
               Last_SQL_Error: Error 'Duplicate entry '3' for key 'test_break_re
pl_idx'' on query. Default database: 'test'. Query: 'insert into test_break_repl
 values (3)'
1 row in set (0.00 sec)
```

**Screen-shot 21—10: Show slave status demonstrating SQL error**

## 21.4.2 SQL Error due to missing database object

If slave database is missing an object and master attempts to replicate log events related to that event, then slave SQL thread will fail with SQL Error 1146.

```
mysql> show slave status\G
*************************** 1. row ***************************
               Slave_IO_State: Waiting for master to send event
                  Master_Host: mobilestatisticsprofessor.com
                  Master_User: repl
                  Master_Port: 3306
                Connect_Retry: 60
              Master_Log_File: mysql-bin.000008
          Read_Master_Log_Pos: 419
               Relay_Log_File: mysqld-relay-bin.000002
                Relay_Log_Pos: 243
        Relay_Master_Log_File: mysql-bin.000008
             Slave_IO_Running: Yes
            Slave_SQL_Running: No
              Replicate_Do_DB:
          Replicate_Ignore_DB:
           Replicate_Do_Table:
       Replicate_Ignore_Table:
      Replicate_Wild_Do_Table:
  Replicate_Wild_Ignore_Table:
                   Last_Errno: 1146
                   Last_Error: Error 'Table 'test.break_sql_thread' doesn't exis
t' on query. Default database: 'test'. Query: 'insert into break_sql_thread valu
es (1)'
                 Skip_Counter: 0
          Exec_Master_Log_Pos: 312
              Relay_Log_Space: 506
              Until_Condition: None
               Until_Log_File:
                Until_Log_Pos: 0
           Master_SSL_Allowed: No
           Master_SSL_CA_File:
           Master_SSL_CA_Path:
              Master_SSL_Cert:
            Master_SSL_Cipher:
               Master_SSL_Key:
        Seconds_Behind_Master: NULL
Master_SSL_Verify_Server_Cert: No
                Last_IO_Errno: 0
                Last_IO_Error:
               Last_SQL_Errno: 1146
               Last_SQL_Error: Error 'Table 'test.break_sql_thread' doesn't exis
t' on query. Default database: 'test'. Query: 'insert into break_sql_thread valu
es (1)'
```

Screen-shot 21—11: SQL Error due to missing database object

## 21.5 Summary

This chapter presented how to interpret slave status as well as common I/O and SQL errors.

# 22 Understanding output of *show processlist*

MySQL command *show processlist* displays a roster of all the running processes. This chapter presents the screenshots from master and slaves. A master replicates to two slaves in this configuration.

Three MySQL Servers located on a LAN. MySQL-Node-1 is master of MySQL-Node-2 and MySQL-Node-3. The roles of the servers and server IP address and hostnames are presented below.

| Srl. No. | Hostname | IP Address | server _id | Role |
|---|---|---|---|---|
| 1 | MySQL-Node-1 | 169.168.11.104 | 11 | Master of MySQL-Node-2 Master of MySQL-Node-3 |
| 2 | MySQL-Node-2 | 169.168.1.141 | 10 | Slave of MySQL-Node-1 |
| 3 | MySQL-Node-3 | 169.168.1.101 | 3000 | Slave of MySQL-Node-1 |

**Table 22—1: Master-2 Slaves Replication Configuration**

Master and 2 slaves configuration physical architecture diagram is presented below.

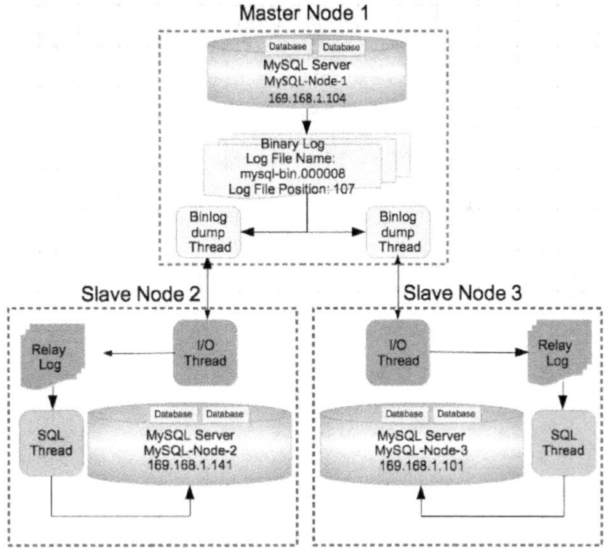


**Figure 22—1: Master and 2 slaves replication configuration**

## 22.1 Processlist from master MySQL-Node-1 when no slaves have established connection to master

```
mysql> show processlist\G
*************************** 1. row ***************************
     Id: 3
   User: root
   Host: MySQL-Node-2:50385
     db: NULL
Command: Query
   Time: 0
  State: NULL
   Info: show processlist
1 row in set (0.01 sec)
```

Screen-shot 22—1: Show processlist command executed on master MySQL-Node-1 when no slave has established connection

When *show processlist* is executed on master when no slave has established connection, the show process query process is listed.

## 22.2 Processlist from slave MySQL-Node-2 when slave process has not started

When *show processlist* command is executed on slave when slave has not started, the show process query process is listed.

```
mysql> show processlist\G
*************************** 1. row ***************************
     Id: 10
   User: root
   Host: MySQL-Node-2:50384
     db: NULL
Command: Query
   Time: 0
  State: NULL
   Info: show processlist
1 row in set (0.00 sec)
```

Screen-shot 22—2: Show processlist command executed on slave MySQL-Node-2 when slave has not started

## 22.3 Processlist from slave MySQL-Node-2 after slave process has started

When *show processlist* command is executed on slave when slave has started, two additional processes listed. Slave I/O process is *process id 11* in the screenshot below which is waiting for master to send event. Slave SQL process is *process id 17* which has read the entire relay log and waiting for the slave I/O thread to update it.

```
mysql> show processlist\G
*************************** 1. row ***************************
     Id: 10
   User: root
   Host: MySQL-Node-2:50384
     db: NULL
Command: Query
   Time: 0
  State: NULL
   Info: show processlist
*************************** 2. row ***************************
     Id: 11
   User: system user
   Host:
     db: NULL
Command: Connect
   Time: 101
  State: Waiting for master to send event
   Info: NULL
*************************** 3. row ***************************
     Id: 12
   User: system user
   Host:
     db: NULL
Command: Connect
   Time: 17
  State: Slave has read all relay log; waiting for the slave I/O thread to updat
e it
   Info: NULL
3 rows in set (0.00 sec)
```

Screen-shot 22—3: Show processlist command executed on slave MySQL-Node-2 after slave started

Table listing the processes is presented below.

| Srl. No. | Server | Role | Master Binlog Dump Process ID | Slave I/O Process ID | Slave SQL Process ID |
|---|---|---|---|---|---|
| 1 | MySQL-Node-1 | Master | | | |
| 2 | MySQL-Node-2 | Slave | | **11** | **17** |
| 3 | MySQL-Node-3 | Slave | | | |

Table 22—2: Processes after slave started on slave MySQL-Node-2

## 22.4 Processlist from master MySQL-Node-1 after slave MySQL-Node-2 established connection

When *show processlist* command is executed on master when a slave has started, an additional process listed. Binlog Dump *process id 4* started after slave established connection to master. This process has sent all binlog to slave.

```
mysql> show processlist\G
*************************** 1. row ***************************
     Id: 3
   User: root
   Host: MySQL-Node-2:50385
     db: NULL
Command: Query
   Time: 0
  State: NULL
   Info: show processlist
*************************** 2. row ***************************
     Id: 4
   User: repl
   Host: MySQL-Node-2:50415
     db: NULL
Command: Binlog Dump
   Time: 7
  State: Master has sent all binlog to slave; waiting for binlog to be updated
   Info: NULL
2 rows in set (0.00 sec)
```

**Screen-shot 22—4: Show processlist command executed on master MySQL-Node-1 after slave MySQL-Node-2 has established connection**

Table listing the processes is presented below.

| Srl. No. | Server | Role | Master Binlog Dump Process ID | Slave I/O Process ID | Slave SQL Process ID |
|---|---|---|---|---|---|
| 1 | MySQL-Node-1 | Master | **4** | | |
| 2 | MySQL-Node-2 | Slave | | 11 | 17 |
| 3 | MySQL-Node-3 | Slave | | | |

Table 22—3: Master and slave processes after slave MySQL-Node-2 started

## 22.5 Processlist from slave MySQL-Node-3 after slave started

When *show processlist* command is executed on slave when slave has started, two additional processes listed. Slave I/O process is *process id 4* in the screenshot below which is waiting for master to send event. Slave SQL process is *process id 5* which has read the entire relay log and waiting for the slave I/O thread to update it.

```
mysql> show processlist\G
*********************** 1. row ***********************
     Id: 3
   User: root
   Host: MySQL-Node-2:50491
     db: NULL
Command: Query
   Time: 0
  State: init
   Info: show processlist
*********************** 2. row ***********************
     Id: 4
   User: system user
   Host:
     db: NULL
Command: Connect
   Time: 384
  State: Waiting for master to send event
   Info: NULL
*********************** 3. row ***********************
     Id: 5
   User: system user
   Host:
     db: NULL
Command: Connect
   Time: 339
  State: Slave has read all relay log; waiting for the slave I/O thread to updat
e it
   Info: NULL
3 rows in set (0.86 sec)
```

Screen-shot 22—5: Show processlist executed on slave MySQL-Node-3 after slave started

Table listing the processes is presented below.

| Srl. No. | Server | Role | Master Binlog Dump Process ID | Slave I/O Process ID | Slave SQL Process ID |
|---|---|---|---|---|---|
| 1 | MySQL-Node-1 | Master | 4 | | |
| 2 | MySQL-Node-2 | Slave | | 11 | 17 |
| 3 | MySQL-Node-3 | Slave | | 4 | 5 |

Table 22—4: Master and slave processes after 2 slaves started

## 22.6 Processlist from master MySQL-Node-1 after slave MySQL-Node-2 and MySQL-Node-3 established connection.

When *show processlist* command is executed on master when two slaves have started, 2 Binlog Dump processes (*process id 4* and 5) started. Both have sent all binlog to slave.

```
mysql> show processlist\G
*********************** 1. row ***********************
     Id: 3
   User: root
   Host: MySQL-Node-2:50385
     db: NULL
Command: Query
   Time: 0
  State: NULL
   Info: show processlist
*********************** 2. row ***********************
     Id: 4
   User: repl
   Host: MySQL-Node-2:50415
     db: NULL
Command: Binlog Dump
   Time: 586
  State: Master has sent all binlog to slave; waiting for binlog to be updated
   Info: NULL
*********************** 3. row ***********************
     Id: 5
   User: repl
   Host: MySQL-Node-3:49211
     db: NULL
Command: Binlog Dump
   Time: 1
  State: Master has sent all binlog to slave; waiting for binlog to be updated
   Info: NULL
3 rows in set (0.00 sec)
```

**Screen-shot 22—6: Show processlist command executed on master MySQL-Node-1 after slaves MySQL-Node-2 and MySQL-Node-3 have established connection**

Table listing the processes is presented below.

| Srl. No. | Server | Role | Master Binlog Dump Process ID | Slave I/O Process ID | Slave SQL Process ID |
|---|---|---|---|---|---|
| 1 | MySQL-Node-1 | Master | 4<br>5 | | |
| 2 | MySQL-Node-2 | Slave | | 11 | 17 |
| 3 | MySQL-Node-3 | Slave | | 4 | 5 |

Table 22—5: Master and slave processes after 2 slaves established connection

## 22.7 Summary

This chapter described the output of *show processlist*; especially, master Binlog Dump and slave I/O as well as Slave SQL processes after slave started.

# 23 Including and excluding databases and tables from replication

MySQL allows replicating certain databases and tables as well as restricting replicating certain other databases and tables. Options available to include and exclude tables and databases are, replicate_do_db, replicate_do_table, replicate_ignore_db and replicate_ignore_table. These options can be specified in MySQL configuration file my.cnf. These need to be specified in the my.cnf file of the slave MySQL server.

## 23.1 replicate_do_db

The list of included databases can be specified by replicate_do_db parameter with one database specified in each line.

An example of including customer and order database in replication is provided below.

```
replicate_do_db=customer
replicate_do_db=order
```

## 23.2 replicate_do_table

The list of included tables can be specified by replicate_do_table parameter with one table specified in each line. Table name needs to be qualified with database name.

An example of including address table of customer database and price table of order database in replication is provided below.

```
replicate_do_table=customer.address
replicate_do_db=order.price
```

## 23.3 replicate_ignore_db

The list of excluded databases can be specified by replicate_ignore_db parameter with one database specified in each line.

An example of excluding mysql, information_schema and performance_schema databases from replication is provided below.

```
replicate_ignore_db=mysql
replicate_ignore_db=information_schema
replicate_ignore_db=performance_schema
```

## 23.4 replicate_ignore_table

The list of excluded tables can be specified by replicate_do_table parameter with one table specified in each line.  Table name needs to be qualified with database name.

An example of excluding user table from mysql database and tables from information_schema database from replication is provided below. This would allow replication not to replicate these tables even if other tables are updated in the same statement.

replicate_ignore_table=mysql.user
replicate_do_db=information_schema.tables


## 23.5 Summary

This chapter explained how to include and exclude databases and tables from replication.

# *24* Interpreting binary and relay log files using *mysqlbinlog*

MySQL provides *mysqlbinlog* utility to read and present binary and relay log files in human readable format. Start and end time of each log event and contents of the log event are presented when mysqlbinlog command reads logs and relay log files. The primary purpose of this utility is to provide transactions to apply to facilitate point-in-time recovery from a database crash.

The lines starting with #at indicates the staring log position. The second line after #at indicate present the date and timestamp and the server id of the server were the event originated from.

## 24.1  Reading binary log

The following mysqlbinlog command is issued to read binary log file mysql-bin.000008. Server id 2 is the master server replicating to server id 1.

### *$mysqlbinlog –uroot –p mysql-bin.000008*

The output of the mysqlbinlog command is presented below.

```
/*!40019 SET @@session.max_insert_delayed_threads=0*/;
/*!50003 SET @OLD_COMPLETION_TYPE=@@COMPLETION_TYPE,COMPLETION_TYPE=0*/;
DELIMITER /*!*/;
# at 4
#140520  7:50:06 server id 1  end_log_pos 106   Start: binlog v 4, server
v 5.1.
52-log created 140520  7:50:06
# Warning: this binlog is either in use or was not closed properly.
BINLOG '
fk97Uw8BAAAAZgAAAGoAAAABAAQANS4xLjUyLWxvZwAAAAAAAAAAAAAAAAAAAAAAAAAAAAAA
AA
AAAAAAAAAAAAAAAAAAAAAAEzgNAAgAEgAEBAQEgAAUwAEGggAAAICAgC
'/*!*/;
# at 106
#140520  7:50:27 server id 1  end_log_pos 134    Intvar
SET INSERT_ID=28/*!*/;
# at 134
#140520  7:50:27 server id 1  end_log_pos
241   Query   thread_id=602   exec_tim
e=0     error_code=0
use test/*!*/;
SET TIMESTAMP=1400590227/*!*/;
SET @@session.pseudo_thread_id=602/*!*/;
SET @@session.foreign_key_checks=1, @@session.sql_auto_is_null=1,
@@session.uniq
ue_checks=1, @@session.autocommit=1/*!*/;
SET @@session.sql_mode=0/*!*/;
SET @@session.auto_increment_increment=3,
```

```
@@session.auto_increment_offset=1/*!*/
;
/*!\C latin1 *//*!*/;
SET
@@session.character_set_client=8,@@session.collation_connection=8,@@sessio
n.
collation_server=8/*!*/;
SET @@session.lc_time_names=0/*!*/;
SET @@session.collation_database=DEFAULT/*!*/;
insert into test_auto_inc values (null)
/*!*/;
# at 241
#140520  7:50:33 server id 1  end_log_pos 269    Intvar
SET INSERT_ID=31/*!*/;
# at 269
#140520  7:50:33 server id 1  end_log_pos
376   Query   thread_id=602   exec_tim
e=0     error_code=0
SET TIMESTAMP=1400590233/*!*/;
insert into test_auto_inc values (null)
/*!*/;
# at 376
#140520  7:50:36 server id 1  end_log_pos 404    Intvar
SET INSERT_ID=34/*!*/;
# at 404
#140520  7:50:36 server id 1  end_log_pos
511   Query   thread_id=602   exec_tim
e=0     error_code=0
SET TIMESTAMP=1400590236/*!*/;
insert into test_auto_inc values (null)
/*!*/;
DELIMITER ;
# End of log file
ROLLBACK /* added by mysqlbinlog */;
/*!50003 SET COMPLETION_TYPE=@OLD_COMPLETION_TYPE*/;
```

At 4, 106, 134, 241, 269, 376 and 404 are the positions in the binary log file where the log
events started.

Log event started at position 404 started on 20th May 2014 at 7:50:36 server time on server
id 1.

## 24.2  Reading relay log

The following mysqlbinlog command is issued to read relay log file mysqld-relay-
bin.000002.

***mysqlbinlog -uroot -p mysqld-relay-bin.000002***

The output of the mysqlbinlog command is presented below. Server id 2 is the master server replicating to server id 1.

```
/*!40019 SET @@session.max_insert_delayed_threads=0*/;
/*!50003 SET @OLD_COMPLETION_TYPE=@@COMPLETION_TYPE,COMPLETION_TYPE=0*/;
DELIMITER /*!*/;
# at 4
#140520  7:55:03 server id 1  end_log_pos 106    Start: binlog v 4, server
v 5.1.
52-log created 140520  7:55:03
BINLOG '
p1B7Uw8BAAAAZgAAAGoAAAAAAQANS4xLjUyLWxvZwAAAAAAAAAAAAAAAAAAAAAAAAAAAAAAA
AA
AAAAAAAAAAAAAAAAAAAAAAAEzgNAAgAEgAEBAQEEgAAUwAEGggAAAAICAgC
'/*!*/;
# at 106
#691231 18:00:00 server id 2  end_log_pos 0      Rotate to mysql-
bin.000009  pos:
98
# at 149
#140520  7:53:16 server id 2  end_log_pos 0      Start: binlog v 4, server
v 5.0.
77-log created 140520  7:53:16
BINLOG '
PFB7Uw8CAAAAXgAAAAAAAAAAAQANS4wLjc3LWxvZwAAAAAAAAAAAAAAAAAAAAAAAAAAAAAAA
AA
AAAAAAAAAAAAAAAAAAAAAAAEzgNAAgAEgAEBAQEEgAASwAEGg==
'/*!*/;
# at 243
#140520  7:55:59 server id 2  end_log_pos 126    Intvar
SET INSERT_ID=14/*!*/;
# at 271
#140520  7:55:59 server id 2  end_log_pos
233   Query    thread_id=1088  exec_tim
e=0     error_code=0
use test/*!*/;
SET TIMESTAMP=1400590559/*!*/;
SET @@session.pseudo_thread_id=1088/*!*/;
SET @@session.foreign_key_checks=1, @@session.sql_auto_is_null=1,
@@session.uniq
ue_checks=1, @@session.autocommit=1/*!*/;
SET @@session.sql_mode=0/*!*/;
SET @@session.auto_increment_increment=3,
@@session.auto_increment_offset=2/*!*/
;
/*!\C latin1 *//*!*/;
SET
@@session.character_set_client=8,@@session.collation_connection=8,@@sessio
n.
collation_server=8/*!*/;
SET @@session.lc_time_names=0/*!*/;
SET @@session.collation_database=DEFAULT/*!*/;
```

```
insert into test_auto_inc values (null)
/*!*/;
DELIMITER ;
# End of log file
ROLLBACK /* added by mysqlbinlog */;
/*!50003 SET COMPLETION_TYPE=@OLD_COMPLETION_TYPE*/;
```

At 4, 106, 149, 243 and 271are the positions in the relay log file where the log events started.

Log event started at position 271 started on 20th May 2014 at 7:55:51 server time on server id 2.

## 24.3 Summary

This chapter demonstrated ways to use mysqlbinlog utility to read and interpret binary and relay log files.

# 25 Troubleshooting and repairing broken replication

The common replication errors encountered along with reasons and remedy are presented below.

| Srl. No. | Type of Error | Error Number | Error Message | Reason | Resolution |
|---|---|---|---|---|---|
| 1 | SQL | 1050 | Duplicate object | Database object exists on slave | |
| 2 | SQL | 1062 | Duplicate key | Master sent a record with a duplicate key | |
| 3 | SQL | 1146 | Missing database object | Database object is not present in slave | |
| 4 | I/O | 1045 | Unable to connect | | |
| 5 | | | | | |
| 6 | | | | | |
| 7 | I/O | 1130 | Host is not allowed to connect | • Firewall issue<br>• Hostname not specified while setting up replication account | • Correct firewall setting to allow slave to connect to master<br>• Recreate replication user with proper slave host detail<br>• Try connecting using host IP address |
| 8 | I/O | 1201 | Could not initialize master info structure | • Old data in master.info<br>• Log file in binary log index could be missing | Execute *reset master* command on master |
| 9 | I/O | 1236 | Checksum error | Mismatching MySQL version | Start master with Binary_log_checksum = NONE |
| 10 | | | Log file name error | Wrong file name | Correct file name |
| 11 | | | Log file position error | Wrong master log position | Correct log position |

| Srl. No. | Type of Error | Error Number | Error Message | Reason | Resolution |
|---|---|---|---|---|---|
| 12 | I/O | 1593 | Duplicate server id | | Correct server_id and restart server |
| 13 | I/O | 2013 | Lost connection | Firewall issue or network issue | Make sure that slave can ping master and connect to master from slave |

Table 25—1: Common replication errors and fixes

Remedy to fix slave issues is to run the following commands after the underlying issue is fixes

*Stop slave*
*Change master*
*Start slave*

Occasionally, *reset slave* and *reset master* commands need to be executed.

## 25.1 Summary

This chapter presented common replication errors and remedies to resolve them.

# 26 Monitoring Replication

Once replication is running, replication process needs to be monitored to ensure that the process is not broken. Both slave I/O and SQL processes need to be monitored. Seconds_behind_master also needs to be monitored to ensure that slave SQL is not falling behind master too much. In the event of SQL or I/O errors, the sooner the problem is detected, the sooner the issue can be resolved. Otherwise, the fix can be resource consuming. MySQL offers show slave status.

The following four parameters need to be monitored and on the event of issues, alert can be sent to an e-mail or SMS can be sent to a cell phone.

- Slave_running: If slave is not running, replication is broken.

- **Last_IO_Errno:** If this field has a value of 0, then slave I/O thread is running fine. Otherwise, slave I/O has an issue.
- **Last_SQL_Errno:** If this field has a value of 0, then slave SQL thread is running fine. Otherwise, slave SQL has an issue.
- **Seconds_behind_master:** If this is beyond the threshold for the organization, then there is an issue with replication performance.

A visual representation of a monitoring process is presented below.

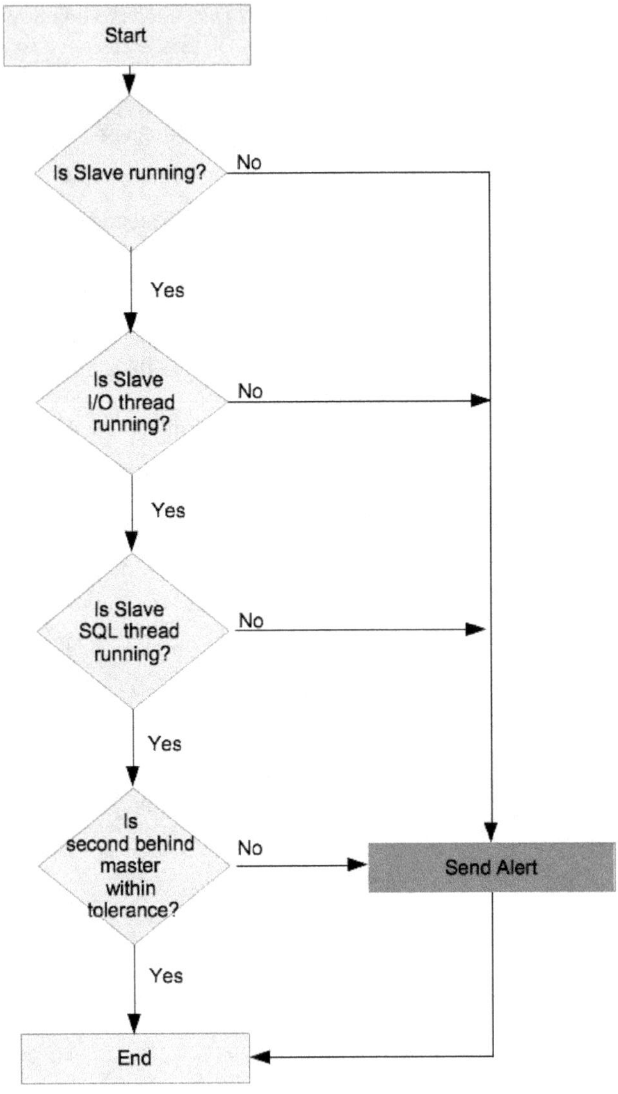


Figure 26—1: Process to monitor replication

The below listed Unix Shell script can be adopted to monitor the replication process.

```
#!/bin/sh

######################################################################
#########
######################################################################
#########
# Name of the Script: Monitor Replication
# Developed by: Business Compass LLC
# Date Developed: May 20, 2014
# Version: 1.0
#
# This script checks whether slave is running, any IO/SQL error has
occurred or slave behind master beyond allowed lag and sends e-mail
based on the following 4 criteria.
# 1. If slave is not running it sends an e-mail
# 2. If Last I/O Error No is not blank
# 3. If Last SQL Error No is not blank
# 4. if Seconds Behind Master is more than 30 minutes
######################################################################
#######

password="password"
emailaddress="monitor-replication@businesscompassllc.com"
slave_lag_behind_master=600 # 10 minutes

# is slave running?
slave_running=`echo "show global status like 'Slave_running'" | mysql
-uroot -p$password  | grep ON | wc -l`


#What is Last IO Error No?
last_io_errno=`echo "show slave status\G" | mysql -uroot -p$password
| grep -i Last_IO_Errno | awk -F": " '{ print $2 }'`

#What is Last SQL Error No?
last_sql_errno=`echo "show slave status\G" | mysql -uroot -p$password
| grep -i Last_SQL_Errno | awk -F": " '{ print $2 }'`

#How far is slave behind master in seconds?
seconds_behind_master=`echo "show slave status\G" | mysql -uroot -
p$password  | grep -i Seconds_Behind_Master | awk -F": " '{ print $2
}'`



if [ $slave_running -eq 0 ]
then
```

```
        hostname=`hostname`;
        date=`date`;

        echo "Check replication - replication off on $hostname at
$date" | mail -s "Replication is off on $hostname at $date"
$emailaddress


else

        if [ $last_io_errno -ne 0 ]
        then

                echo "Check replication - I/O error $last_io_errno
occurred on $hostname at $date" | mail -s "Replication is error
$last_io_errno on $hostname at $date"  $emailaddress
        fi

        if [ $last_sql_errno -ne 0 ]
        then

                echo "Check replication - SQL error $last_sql_errno
occurred on $hostname at $date" | mail -s "Replication is error
$last_sql_errno on $hostname at $date"  $emailaddress
        fi

        if [ $seconds_behind_master -gt $slave_lag_behind_master ]
        then

                echo "Check replication - Seconds Behind Slave
$seconds_behind_slave seconds $hostname at $date is greater than 1/2
hour" | mail -s "Replication is error $last_sql_errno on $hostname at
$date"  $emailaddress
        fi

fi
```

## 26.1 Summary

This chapter presented ways to monitor replication process and send alerts if the process
is broken or slow.